Instructions 1

LET AUGMENTED REALITY CHA

With your smartphone, iPad or tablet you can use the **Hasmark AR** app to invoke the augmented reality experience to literally read outside the book.

1. Download the **Hasmark app** from the **Apple App Store** or **Google Play**

2. Open and select the (vue) option

3. Point your lens at the full image with the and enjoy the augmented reality experience.

Go ahead and try it right now with the Hasmark Publishing International logo.

ENDORSEMENTS

"A wonderful book full of valuable, relatable wisdom. The practical and profound advice continues to resonate with you long after you've finished."

—Judy O'Beirn,
President of Hasmark Publishing International

"Pauline is truly a soul's cheerleader! Though her advice of "just trust" is simple, it isn't always easy to do, so she shows you how through the lessons she mines from her life's ups and downs. As a coach, wise friend, and teacher, she knows which life lesson you are facing, as she has faced it too. She offers insights and tools to hold yourself accountable and upgrade your mindset. She is the teacher who will appear when you are ready to live your best life."

—Sarah McLean,
Bestselling Author of *Soul-Centered,*
Transform Your Life in 8 Weeks with Meditation and
The Power of Attention

"Your intuition is the biggest gift you have. Pauline helps you connect more deeply into your inner wisdom so that you can live a truly purpose driven and fulfilling life."

—Susie Moore,
Bestselling Author of *Let It Be Easy*

"You will find inspiration in this fabulous book. Allow Pauline's guidance to lift you up to a higher level of consciousness. I love Pauline Rohdich's book, *Just Trust*, as it is an authentic and inspiring read."

—Peggy McColl,
New York Times Bestselling Author
http://PeggyMcColl.com

"Pauline has done a phenomenal job sharing the universal truth that trusting your intuition can transform every aspect of your life. Her message is uplifting and reflected deeply in her own life story. I am so proud that she is an RTT therapist."

—Marisa Peer,
Creator of Rapid Transformational
Therapy and Bestselling Author

'With Just Trust! Pauline Rohdich has found her true purpose and she is passionate about helping others find theirs.'

— Edel Coffey
Number One Bestselling
Author of *Breaking Point*

Dear Clare

Just
TRUST!

Listen to the wisdom of your soul...
it knows the way.

lots of love
Paulie
x

Pauline Rohdich

Hasmark
PUBLISHING
INTERNATIONAL

Editor: Day Bulger
Proofreader: Harshita Sharma harshita@hasmarkpublishing.com
Cover Design: Anne Karklins anne@hasmarkpublishing.com
Interior Layout: Amit Dey amit@hasmarkpublishing.com

ISBN 13: 978-1-77482-061-2
ISBN 10: 1774820617

CONTENTS

DEDICATION

To Finn, thank you for being the greatest gift
in my life. You can be whatever you
believe yourself to be. Just Trust.

FOREWORD

Without stepping outside your door, you can be bombarded with messages from all around the world about what you should think, how you should dress, who you should idolize, and where you should spend your money.

We're flooded with constant messages about how we should live our lives—like the classic two kids, a dog, and a home with the picket fence dream, or the idea that you should strive as hard as you can for financial gain. And you should do all this while maintaining a Hollywood-style fitness regimen and never aging!

Millions of people are awakening to the realization that the options we're "sold" for life just don't work. In fact, they often lead to breakdowns in physical health, mental health, relationships, finances, or career.

People are hungry for alternative ways to live their lives. So where can you turn to find guidance?

The answer is to trust the messages coming from your own soul.

This is not as easy as it sounds. The messages from your soul are competing with a myriad of limiting beliefs and fears in your subconscious mind. In fact, the messages from your soul can be very threatening to your previous ways of living, thinking, and working.

That's why this book, *Just Trust,* is so needed right now. In it, Pauline Rohdich clearly shows you how to cut through the noise so you can hear your soul and develop the courage to act on it.

For many years, Pauline has had a deep passion to help people live their most aligned lives. This theme of service is evident throughout her varied background, which includes working in the police force in Ireland, as a flight attendant, an energy healer, a life coach, a hypnotherapist, and a yoga and meditation teacher.

In the writing of this book, Pauline shares her true voice and calling: to guide people worldwide to live lives with greater authenticity, fulfillment, and joy. (That's what can happen through listening to your soul.)

Personally, I can attest that the greatest achievements, synchronicities, and miracles in my life have come from listening to the wisdom of my soul. This includes my experience sitting in a silent meditation retreat and getting the idea for *Chicken Soup for the Woman's Soul.* Thank goodness I trusted my soul, because this idea led to me becoming a multiple-time #1 *New York Times* best-selling author and forever changed my life. I've continued to listen to my soul since then, and the miracles have continued too!

Pauline is an inspiring example of someone who truly walks her talk. I had the joy of meeting Pauline when she listened to the voice of her soul and became one of my first Happy for No Reason Certified Trainers, spreading the message of happiness around the world. I've been honored to witness her using the principles she teaches in her own life—living aligned with her heart and soul. This approach has brought her compassion, wisdom, clarity, and fulfilling success.

I'm thrilled she's sharing the important messages in this powerful book, and I know that anybody who opens to and follows her guidance will have a shift in their life toward greater joy, happiness, and love.

—Marci Shimoff,
#1 *New York Times* Bestselling
Author of *Happy for No Reason* and
Chicken Soup for the Woman's Soul

TUNING IN TO YOUR INNER VOICE

When I run after what I think I want, my days are a furnace of stress and anxiety; if I sit in my own place of patience, what I need flows to me, and without pain. From this I understand that what I want also wants me, is looking for me and attracting me. There is a great secret here for anyone who can grasp it.

—Rumi

My Miracle Baby

How glad I am that I trusted my inner voice, the whispers of my soul, to achieve the one thing that was unquestionable for me. You bet I am! You see, I used to joke that I'd have eaten coal if it meant I would hold a baby in my arms, and I probably would have.

On the third of January at seven minutes past four, I gave birth to my precious son, Finn, and proved that anything is possible once you have faith and trust and allow love infused with unshakeable belief to lead the way. He is my miracle baby; I believe I was divinely guided every step of the way because I expected him with all my heart and soul. My years of fascination with the law of attraction were proven, and it was at this moment that I became much more aware of this law consciously. Despite being told on numerous occasions that it was unlikely that I would have a baby, my desire to become a mother never waned; I trusted I'd be granted my greatest wish. I knew I had to do the invisible work of using my imagination to visualize my desired outcome. I did it obsessively, and that's what made the difference.

Miracles were always something that I believed in, and in the past fifteen years, the work of Helen Schucman and William Thetford in their metaphysical book, *A Course in Miracles*, inspired my original fascination. The course teaches that miracles occur naturally as expressions of love. A miracle is a shift in our inner perception, being willing to turn fear-based thoughts into love-based ones. I was willing to do whatever it took to become the one thing I wanted to be more than anything else in the world—a mother. Therefore, I put my order into the benevolent universe, describing my future baby in great detail, right down to his personality and characteristics. And yes, I can tell you, I got what I asked for. There was no place for fear with this intention. I was totally in awe of the idea of motherhood.

Let's go back to the start of this journey more than twenty years earlier, where I was sitting in the doctor's surgery, a teenager awaiting her fate. The doctor came in and sat down. He asked me a few questions, and after a while, made the declaration, "Pauline, I don't think you will ever be able to have children."

A tsunami of confusion washed over me as I took in his words. How could this be true? Surely, he was mistaken. I was eighteen years old, full of dreams, one of which was to mother a brood much like my own family. I walked out of the surgery that day and felt so alone but deep in thought. Questions such as, "How could he make such a prediction? Was there something wrong with my body? Was I damaged goods?" whirled around in my head. And the scariest question of all was "Who would marry me?" This internal monologue continued until I turned the corner to my home, and then something magical happened. It wasn't so much a voice in my head but a feeling in my heart, like a jolt of electricity that lifted my spirits and put a pep in my step, making me believe that my dream of motherhood would be achieved, no matter what anyone said.

Not unlike many people at this time, I was raised to revere the medical profession and accept its opinion as gospel. However, I'd begun to question the opinions of others, and I knew inside that I needed to make my own mind up about things. I began to recognize that some of the things I'd seen and was being told were not true in other areas of my life, and again, this led me to question deeper. I doubted what the doctor told me, and little did I know in that moment of doubt that a miracle was taking place then and there. I recognized that if I wanted to accomplish something that was in my heart to do, then it was my responsibility and no one else's. Often described as headstrong, I think I was more *heartstrong*. The credo "make my own mind up" had become significant. I believe that is precisely what we must do every day to live our best lives and to trust that we can make up our own minds while honoring the wish within our hearts. I decided not to take on board what the doctor told me in his office that day. I didn't accept it as fact, and I started to believe that I had some control over my destiny. I began to ride this wonderful wave of hope and belief in myself from this time of my life onwards.

Trusting the Power of My Inner Voice

This book describes my experiences as a spiritual seeker on a mission to uncover the purpose of my life and its meaning. Along the way, I learned to trust my inner voice and innate wisdom to guide me when the odds seemed stacked against me. I've been led to teachers who've helped me make sense of my inquiring mind and understand the truth of "who I am" and "why I am". I've experienced the power of leading from the love within my heart to reconcile the challenges I have faced in my life. In sharing my story and insights, my wish is not to tell you what to do with your life but to hopefully empower you to know that you always have access to infinite wisdom in the form of your intuition, or inner voice.

"What is the inner voice?" I hear you ask. Well, I like to describe it as the voice of our soul or the voice of truth, and since each of us is a spiritual being living temporarily in a physical body, it then becomes the voice of our *authentic Self.* Sometimes, it's referred to as inner wisdom or a gut feeling, an instinct, or a sixth sense. Maybe you've called it your intuition or higher Self. It doesn't matter what you call it, but know that it's part of you and has been there since you were born. Intuition is the highest form of intelligence, allowing you to access knowledge and insights from the field of infinite possibilities. It is one of our higher mental faculties, and everyone can learn to hone it.

When you use your intuition, you gain an immediate understanding of something. You just know, and you know that you know it. It's a feeling that arises that very few can describe accurately in words. Still, it can change the direction of your life in a heartbeat—just like in that moment when I heard a whisper and knew instinctively not to let the doctor's suggestion, that I would probably not be able to have children, become a fact in my own life. It's as if you can see from the inside out—an inner sight giving you an awareness and understanding of what's possible.

Even if you've been unaware of or out of touch with your intuition, you can develop the skill of working with it. When we follow our soul's guidance, we can live a rich, divinely inspired life infused with purpose, ease, and grace.

From an early age, I was connected to my soul, but being exposed to a predominantly Catholic upbringing caused me to lose that connection over time. It took more than four decades to have the confidence to speak up and own what I knew deep down. I felt challenged for most of my life, where my identity was in conflict. I reluctantly conformed to what was expected of me. Like most children, I had no say as a child, but I always had a sense of being more than what I saw in the mirror, although it took me a long time to see the "perfect" invisible part of me. This sense allowed me to love and accept my imperfect reflection. My natural curiosity helped me understand that any self-doubt I was feeling in my life was caused by an unconscious denial of my true essence and spirit and a disconnection from the truth.

As I got older, I began a deliberate relationship with my soul, tuning in to my intuition for guidance and direction. I became fascinated with the idea that I could receive or "download" advice from an unseen source that I could rely on to make better decisions in my life rather than asking everyone and anyone for their opinions. I was intrigued when I realized that my childhood inner knowing was alive and well for a time before it was overpowered by doctrine and dogma. I learned that fine-tuning our intuition takes practice and that you must trust its wisdom and listen intently because it always leads you to the most nourishing choice that will benefit all concerned. Our soul is guiding us in every moment towards our future best Self, helping us to remember the promise we made before our incarnation. A promise to serve humanity with our unique gifts and talents.

Thanks to my curiosity and exploration in finding the meaning of my life, I learned that I'm both clairaudient and claircognizant, meaning my intuition communicates to me with clear messages and insights that I can hear or download, at times lightning fast. However, I'm sometimes distracted and overwhelmed just like anyone else, and I forget to pause and go within to my reliable advisor. We all have these abilities. It just takes practice to develop them.

Numerous experiences have advanced my insight and awakening. I've confronted my thoughts, perceptions, and beliefs, and I've re-evaluated my life choices more than once. I soon learned that if I wanted different things—be they material, emotional, physical, or spiritual—I needed to think and act differently. Knowing that my intuition is available as my guide twenty-four seven has helped me in my darker moments. Tuning in to this intuition has helped me make some of the most significant decisions in my life and overcome some of the blunders that could have been avoided had I paid more attention to its guidance.

The Answers Are in the Questions

If you doubt your intuition, as many do, you may find yourself continually asking others for *their* point of view on *your* life. Since we are not taught as children about this gift or the many other superpowers that we each possess, it's understandable that we would doubt the power of intuition to help us make the most necessary decisions.

For those of you who doubt your intuitive abilities, think about times when you had the urge to call someone because you felt something was wrong with them, and then you discovered that you were right. Maybe you had an instant dislike of someone and were wary of their motives, and eventually, you were proven correct when they showed their true colors. What about the times when you got repeated signs that you were on track with something, where you followed those signs and found an opportunity to advance your goal or dream? That was your intuition guiding you.

Other people—parents, teachers, and friends—will tell you what to do and what they think is best for you. In many cases, they have good intentions, but there comes a time when we have to be more discerning about what or who we allow to influence us. The moment you start to mistrust your inner voice by asking others what they think you should do with your life, you have opened the door to doubt, worry, and the potential to destroy your dream. You have lost control of your destiny. You have diluted the potency of your superpower and handed over the responsibility for your life to someone or something else. Whose life are you living? Which lens are you looking through, and whose rules are you obeying? Do you wholeheartedly believe that another person knows what is best for you? I'm not saying that you shouldn't seek professional help when you need to understand yourself more, but I believe the support we all need is to be reminded of our inner power to heal, forgive, trust, thrive, and make nourishing choices.

Therefore, I make a concerted effort to ask my clients more questions about their dilemmas so they can build trust in themselves and begin to find their own solutions. I learned relatively recently that *the answers are in the questions.* Think about it. When you ask yourself a good question, the answer surfaces like magic, except it's not magic; it's your soul communicating through whatever channel is open to receive its message. The answer might not come straight away, but you'll either feel it, hear it, see it, or know it. You may even be given a sign that you've been answered. I often ask for a sign from the universe to let me know if I'm doing the right thing. It's so comforting when you receive one. It could be a white feather on my path in the most unlikely of places or a message on a random page in a book. I might hear a song that speaks to my soul, and I know that I'm on track. I ask, "Give me a sign that I'm going in the right direction," and then I expect to receive it.

Trusting Intuition as a Sacred Practice

For me, trusting in my inner voice is a sacred practice and is strengthened by meditation, mindfulness, and prayer. When you get still and centered, the outside noise and chaos subside, and you can tap into the pure essence of your soul. Withdrawing from the outside world's demands, hype, and manipulation allows you to become more in tune with your highest, wisest Self. You can receive the answers you seek and the guidance you crave and know what's right for you from this place. When you are in the zone of absolute faith in your intuition, you feel guided, and you receive a metaphorical thumbs-up with many delightful, deliberate coincidences revealed to you. I cherish what the late spiritual author Dr. Wayne Dyer pointed out about the words *listen* and *silent*; they each contain the same letters. We need to be silent to listen. Isn't that powerful?

Similarly, it has been said that when we pray, we are talking to God, and when we meditate, God is talking to us. This lights me up and elevates my faith, hope, and belief on this co-creative journey.

All my young life, I was exposed to the concept of prayer as putting on a holy, expressionless face and squeezing my eyes shut while repeating words that made no sense to me. The prayers suggested I was a sinner who had to beg for forgiveness lest I burn in the fires of hell unless I repented, and even then, I might still end up in limbo or purgatory. Even as a child, I felt strongly that such fear and dread should not be programmed into any child. I was more afraid of the incorrect information being taught to us and its impact. It was as if we had to apologize for our existence, and I was acutely aware of the damage it was doing as I was brought to my knees daily to say those prayers in silent despair.

I always had faith and absolute trust in what I couldn't see but what I could feel. Deep down, I seemed to know that someday there would be a more open conversation about the damage of such an introduction to God. I knew there would be an awakening of consciousness that would lead us to recognize the truth more easily.

Today, I love to pray to God in my own words, directly from my heart, and inspired by whatever I'm feeling at the moment. I don't need to go into a church to pray to God. I'm just as comfortable being in a temple, mosque, or synagogue. I have experienced being in all these places and being able to pray with ease without fearing any condemnation. I'm often closest to God when I'm simply gazing at a sunset or absorbing the sunlight through the trees, but it was at a whole other level when my son was born. I felt the presence of God as I held him for the first time. My wish had been granted. I was holding in my arms the evidence of a mind, heart, and soul aligned with a purpose to mother with absolute faith and zero doubt.

I'd been given a chance to share my understanding of God with my son, and all I ever wanted was that he would know unconditional love, be open to everything, and make his own mind up as he got older. Of course, I enjoy reminding him from time to time of how "lucky" he is to have a mother who never gave up on her dream of having her child. Needless to say, there's much eye-rolling and shoulder shrugging, but deep down, I feel I've instilled in him the benefit of being tenacious and believing in himself.

Meditation rescued me from a period in my life where I felt alone and unsure of my next moves. I had lost my sense of purpose, which was scary as I always seemed to know what I wanted to do and where I wanted to be. I found a much deeper connection with God and the universe when I meditated than when I prayed.

My practice begins with gratitude and my intentions as I visualize my dreams and goals. I trust that whatever guidance is meant for me will be fully revealed when it is ready to be revealed to me. Many styles of meditation exist, and I believe it's essential to find the one that resonates best with you. The one I favor and teach is mantra-based and dates to the Vedas of India, more than five thousand years ago. Repeating a mantra allows you to anchor down in your meditation so that when your mind drifts or you get caught up with your thoughts, you become aware of this and can simply return to repeating your mantra. The goal of meditation is to experience your soul in the silence and stillness of your being. However, I have found many benefits from the more dynamic meditations in recent years, such as walking meditations, viewing yoga as a meditation in motion, and creative visualizations using the power of my imagination. Regardless of which one you choose, when you surrender to the practice over time, you glimpse your soul and know that whatever guidance you receive is reliable and personal.

Tuning In to the Universal Intelligence

There is something that is encouraging us to expand, and it's the same something that's growing our hair, making us breathe, and giving us ideas to move us out of our dissatisfaction and motivate us. We must become acquainted and learn to communicate with this something that I call *God* or *Spirit*. I also refer to it as *energy* or *universal intelligence*. You may have another name for it, but I'm confident we're referring to the same invisible power that animates our very being, which is omnipotent and available to everyone simultaneously.

When we get the idea that we are connected to a higher intelligence, an invisible power that operates twenty-four seven, we can feel comfortable wanting more from life and assume that life wants more from us. The secret is to know that you are not alone in creating your life; the unseen forces of God and the universe are co-creating with you. You must keep an open mind and heart to trust what you cannot see. Absence of evidence is not evidence of absence, and when you look back on your life, you'll find much evidence of God.

Some people refer to life as a game, and if we are to win, we need to know the rules. Knowing how to work with the universal intelligence to manifest a beautiful life becomes our game plan. Throughout this book, I highlight my journey to a new, higher level of understanding of how this life game works, where uncovering my life purpose and being a conduit of peace, love, and joy has always been important to me. Ultimately, doing what I've been put on Earth to do is what gets me out of bed, to study and grow into the best version of myself. Learning and sharing knowledge and ancient wisdom are at the heart of who I am, and helping people to achieve true success has become my passionate purpose.

Understanding the Universal Laws

Universal laws are working this life game, and we can learn to use them to our advantage. We must first identify who we are at our core and why we want what we want. The more awake and aware we become, the more we align with our spirit and the intelligence of life itself, moving us progressively in the direction of our dreams. Alongside the idea that what you want wants you, in the words of the wonderful Deepak Chopra, "are the *mechanics* for fulfilling every desire." In other words, each dream or desire you have means that you have the right to it and the ability to achieve it. The *how* to achieve it is built into the desire, and it's not our job to know what that might look like. It is our job to stay in the good energy of our dreams so that everything we need—all the resources, money, people, and circumstances—shows up in our lives to make this a reality. We need to use our imagination to see ourselves in possession of our dream fulfilled and, most importantly, to see how having achieved it makes us *feel*, and as Neville Goddard states, "feeling is the secret."

In my work, I often hear people talk about those who appear to "have it all," the "lucky few" who were born on the right side of the street with the silver spoon and advantages that go way beyond money, status, and good looks. I used to feel that there was some truth to this, but now I believe that we continuously create our luck by being prepared for life's opportunities. And that's what luck is, preparation and opportunity coming together. We prepare by studying ourselves through personal and spiritual development to understand how powerful we are.

Knowing this, in turn, helps our confidence to grow, and we begin to realize that we are capable of much more than we were led to believe. Some say that we don't need luck when there's law. The laws of the universe are at our disposal always; we just have to learn how to obey them. Working with the laws is the way to ensure your "luck" and guarantee the outcome that you seek.

Finding Your Purpose: What's For You Will Never Pass You By

> *When you are born, your work is placed*
> *in your heart.*

> —Kahlil Gibran

This quote reflects what was mentioned earlier, the recognition that when our awakening accelerates, we will begin to know the truth of who we are and know that the fear-mongering and domination of dogmatic ideologies should be challenged. Sometimes, this truth is revealed in a quote, a poem, a speech, or a book. We're pre-coded at birth, and we must crack the code over our lives to carry out our mission on Earth. We're born for a reason and are here for a purpose, and we must find out what that reason is. My greatest fear for many years was that I would not fulfill mine and ultimately betray my soul.

The journey of uncovering our purpose is never-ending because it evolves as we do. My purpose shifted when I became a mother, which remains for me the highest purpose to honor. Even though I wasn't told I was having a boy, I just knew I was having a boy. We had chosen his name, Finn Isaac, months earlier, and it fit him perfectly. Despite the devastation I felt when I lost his twin earlier in my pregnancy and the three other miscarriages over the years, everything I could have hoped for was now in my arms. The emptiness and longing were now filled with a palpable love I'd never known before. In a matter of seconds, as I absorbed this precious child, I saw the miracle of creation, the perfection of this little being, the many faces of his ancestors in his own, the gift I'd been given, the responsibility of raising him, and the reminder that this baby was a wise soul in a fresh, new body. I knew my greatest challenge would be helping him preserve such wisdom and awareness without destroying his spirit and sense of self.

I was familiar with the poem "On Children" from *The Prophet* by Kahlil Gibran, where he wrote that our children are not our children; they come through us but not from us. And though they are with us, they do not belong to us. We can give them our love but not our thoughts because they have their own. I knew I had to remember this idea because I had an opportunity to practice it with this precious soul, whom I believed would be one of my greatest teachers. I felt honored and privileged to have received the gift of motherhood, even though I'd had to wait longer than most of my friends before it was my turn. I was so ready. Being the best for my son became my goal, and supporting him in becoming all he could be became my mission and purpose.

Recently, when I was writing about purpose, an exciting thing happened, not for the first time. I had taken a break and had run myself a wonderfully nourishing mid-morning bubble bath infused with all the delights that would soothe my achy muscles and relax my busy mind. Just as I took a sigh of relief, my phone spontaneously started to play some music. Initially startled, I then smiled and said a silent *thank you*. I knew I was being told to relax. The title of the piece was "Mind Massage," and it was perfect for the occasion. I had no idea that this song was on any playlist, but I accepted the synchronistic message I was receiving. It was then followed by a song that I associate with my dad, "Secret Love" by Doris Day. My dad often called me Doris Day, but I know he saw me as a Calamity Jane, a no-nonsense, direct, but fun-loving teen who asked too many difficult questions, which you'll hear more about later.

There I was, lathered in lavender and peppermint bubbles, and I started singing along. Suddenly, the lyrics had a new meaning. They weren't the words about a 1950s romance. Instead, they represented my secret desire to share a more important and meaningful mission in the world.

I can barely sing those words without breaking down in tears. They mean so much to me: the song itself, the fabulous Doris Day, the movies I watched with my dad, and the years of suppressing my secret message. My secret love is about honoring my life's true purpose and the work placed in my heart at my birth. I became impatient to speak out about that and share the message with others. Simply put, I want everyone to know that they have a purpose and that they shouldn't hide away any longer. Don't be a best-kept secret! It's time to move from feeling invisible to invincible, and I want to help others make that transition in less time than it took me.

Can you feel that truth for yourself?

Our life's purpose is to remember who we are at our core and know that we each have a promise to fulfill. It's to uncover our gifts and talents so that we can contribute to and serve humanity in our unique way. It's about learning from our mistakes and reaching our potential, doing what we love, and being paid to do it without feeling like we're working. It's about awakening to our higher Self while raising our awareness about what's possible.

I have been reminded many times of the promise I made before I was born to live a full life, one where I can encourage others to do the same and to bring joy to as many people as possible. I promised to teach and share about love and forgiveness from a place of integrity and compassion, to remind others to filter the truth from the lies that hold them back so they can reach their potential. What did you promise?

It can take many disappointments and misses before we wake up and realize that we're off track from what we're best equipped to do with our life. Being willing to see dissatisfaction with life as a creative state can motivate us to transform our circumstances.

For many, myself included, we can know that we want to help others, but the big question becomes, "In what way can I do that?" This is when some introspection is required and is sometimes referred to as the *inner work*. For many of us, this investigative fact-finding mission happens only after we've had enough of going around in circles with more questions than answers, blindfolded and impervious to our magnificence and the work that was coded into our hearts when we were born.

Without question, there is a purpose for our physical existence on this earthly plane. I believe that when we are born, our memory of our authentic Self becomes blurred, and we spend our life having experiences to help us gain a clearer picture of who we are. When we fully embrace the idea that we are spiritual beings and awaken to the truth that our divinity is in disguise, dwelling temporarily in our physical body with so much power and potential to create a beautiful life, you could say we have solved the mystery of our life.

We get so many opportunities to awaken to our gifts and talents and to answer the question as to how we can help others and serve humanity in our unique way. Often, we are moved to explore more of who we are and ask some critical questions, and sometimes, this occurs following some of life's disappointments and perceived rejections. I learned to see rejection as God's protection, a redirection to something even better, and that idea always feels reassuring and illuminating.

My wise mother, in her attempt to comfort me when I was impatient and in a hurry with my life, told me, "What's for you will never pass you by." That's what the poet Rumi is suggesting in the opening quote, that we don't need to run after what we want in a frenzy. We especially don't need to run after what we *think* we want, but rather live our life from a place of trust, being still and understanding that the guidance we seek will reveal itself. I suffered the most when I was hasty and controlling instead of allowing things to flow more organically. Just pause, surrender to the problem-free zone of the present moment, and trust that a new beginning, a new opportunity, awaits.

We can find clues to uncover our purpose. The evidence is there right from the beginning of our lives. It shows up in the things that we love to do and what we find easy, or sometimes, it reveals itself in the pain and sadness we've endured. Following Robin Roberts's mantra, so many people have "made their mess their message" and have gone on to help others to rise from their pain and suffering. When we pause to inquire within, we are led, and our purpose unfolds spontaneously and gradually. We receive signs from the universe all the time. They might come in the form of a message from a friend, an announcement you might hear on the radio, a poster in the supermarket, or the lyrics in a song. Can you see how that worked for me with good ol' Doris Day? You will identify something common to each sign, nudging you to pay attention and act accordingly.

I also accept that we have many purposes in our lives according to our roles, such as daughter, son, student, parent, employee, and employer. Still, you can do something with your gifts and talents that no one else can do, and that's because no one else is just like you. You have no competition when you're being you. While we're all the same insofar as we've been created from the one energy, we are the individuated aspects of that energy source. You are unique, and you have been born to express your uniqueness fearlessly. I know personally how scary and frustrating it can be, but here's the truth: the thing that will bring you the most fulfillment and joy is often right under your nose. It's the thing that you can do with your eyes closed, the things you are interested in knowing more about. You might not see it initially as your purpose, but maybe you become the go-to person who does this thing so well that you gain notoriety and never have to worry about finances or feeling useless ever again. The clues are there since childhood.

If you are on a quest right now for self-knowledge or uncovering your life purpose, I encourage you to be committed to it. Stay the course despite the ups and downs. No one escapes them, and when you are willing to have a different view of them, you are on your way to creating miracles. I will share with you how numerous factors helped reveal my true purpose over time and why believing that "I am the universe" elevated my confidence and self-belief to a whole other level. I won't pretend that finding my purpose was an easy task, but once I began to look within, it was simple, and I can assure you that it's worth every twist and turn on the road. Enjoy the journey—that's where you'll find the magic.

Getting Out of Your Own Way

You've always known that another way for you to live your life exists. But you've been afraid perhaps to go after it, and that's perfectly understandable. You must train yourself to act upon it and choose to explore the possibilities.

Do you notice that being frustrated with things that are not going your way opens you up to knowing what you don't want, giving rise to an idea of what you do want? Deciding what you're going to do about it, if anything, is like having a tug-of-war inside your mind. We're so afraid of the unknown, and we exhaust ourselves worrying about what might go wrong. For a while, you might ignore your desire and head down the rabbit hole to hide, pretending that you're coping and that you're happy with your lot. Binging on prosecco, retail therapy, food, and the like can only bring us so far. Sooner or later, we must face our demons and surrender to the gentle voice of our wise soul to show us that there is another way.

As we awaken to the realization that we have complete autonomy over our life and the capacity to ask better questions, we become liberated to make more informed decisions that will bring us the peace and happiness we seek. We must start by addressing our self-sabotaging beliefs, primarily formed in early childhood when we were too little and ill-equipped to distinguish between right and wrong, true and false. Our aim is to break free from our self-imposed limitations created over a lifetime. Loosening the grip of societal and institutional misconceptions becomes our focus and *getting out of our own way* becomes the position we must take.

We formed assumptions and came to conclusions based on what we were exposed to and what we witnessed around us. In many cases, we created a negative image of ourselves and allowed it to lead our life. Regardless of whether you have a positive or negative self-image, you are silently communicating a message to the world, and this is bringing you either joy and success or pain and suffering.

I want you to see yourself as a human magnet. Depending on how you feel about yourself and your life, you draw more of the same to you. If you are happy and confident, you will likely attract people and situations that increase your happiness and confidence. On the other hand, if you're sad and lacking confidence, you can expect more of that energy to come to you. You deserve to be happy; it is your birthright and the goal of all goals. It's time to confront what's not true and permit yourself to listen to the truth of the deeper part of you, which you can access when you get still and listen to your heart.

Embracing Failures and Uncertainties along the Way

Remain open to all possibilities, including the idea that something better than you could have imagined for yourself is on its way. Uncertainty is an essential part of life and something many of us struggle with, but the freedom we seek comes when we accept the things we cannot control and look for the opportunity to grow within our problems. A solution to every problem exists. But I know it can be a challenge to loosen the control strings and allow events to unfold, especially if you're anything like me, a recovering control freak! Things usually do work out for the best in the end, and I hope that you agree as you reflect on your own life and its eventual outcomes. As Steve Jobs said, "You can't connect the dots looking forward; you can only connect them looking backwards." So, you have to trust that the dots will somehow connect in your future. You have to trust in something—your gut, destiny, life, karma, whatever. This approach has never let me down, and it has made all the difference in my life."

I'm blessed to have studied with some of the most outstanding teachers and coaches, who helped me join the proverbial dots of my life and find meaning and peace in many of my mistakes and failures. I've been able to see where my strengths are and highlight the areas where a deep-rooted passion fuels my soul's purpose every day. If we learn from our mistakes and see them as part of the process of our evolution, we will be okay. I have learned that it's tough in the beginning and messy in the middle when we are on our way to making changes in our life but always phenomenal on the other side.

Sometimes, we just want to give up. We tell ourselves that it's too complicated and think that the process mustn't be working, and when we get pushed back, that's our cue to stop. If only we'd been taught that change is uncomfortable, that it's normal to want to give up, and that pushing through despite the obstacles turns us into winners in this life game. Much like having surgery, it can be messy; transforming our lives and manifesting our dreams and goals can be confronting and make us want to scurry back to our comfort zone, or as

I like to call it, the danger zone. The surgeon doesn't give up on the patient or walk away from his responsibilities. We, too, must never give up on ourselves and take full responsibility for following through.

As David Guy Powers states, "Success has been defined as the ability to go from failure to failure without losing enthusiasm." Enthusiasm is one of my favorite words. It comes from the Greek word *entheos*, which means "the God within." I believe we are truly successful as long as we remain connected to the God within, our soul, and its mission. For me, success and spirituality are inseparable.

Failures and mistakes are simply feedback and an essential part of our path to success. Believing that life is happening *for* us rather than *to* us moves us from a victim mentality to one where we know we can achieve whatever we want, remembering that when things don't go our way, there is a reason. I'm sure, like me, you've felt rejected by people and life at times. It's a sad state to be in where we overanalyze everything and conclude that something must be wrong with us. As I mentioned earlier, maybe if you can see rejection as God's protection, you might find it easier to celebrate the diversion.

Order Your Coffin

Change is inevitable, nothing ever stays the same; everything evolves. Everything in our world is energy—energy is all there is, and it's always in motion, meaning that it is always looking to move into form. We each can manipulate this energy with our thoughts and feelings and manifest our deepest desires.

This is what I did with my desire to have a baby. It's the same process if you want to buy your dream home, attract the love of your life, or travel the world. We are working with the law of perpetual transmutation of energy, and it's the reason our thoughts become things.

It is important to be aware of your thoughts and feelings as that's what you're creating. This is why when we say things such as, "I love things just the way they are, and I wouldn't change a thing," we are displaying our ignorance of this primary law. I showed my ignorance of this law when I attended a weekly spiritual gathering with other seekers several years ago. Our guide asked each of us about our goals for the future. When she came to me, I was grinning like a Cheshire cat, feeling very satisfied with my lot. My son was two years old, and I was a blissed-out mother enjoying being able to take care of him without also having to worry about juggling a job, thanks to our booming family business at the time. Life was perfect, but I had stopped dreaming for myself, envisioning my son's future instead. I replied to her, "I'm good, I don't need another thing. My life is complete." Naturally, I expected she would move to the next person in the group; instead, she spun around and pointed her finger at me and told me in no uncertain terms to order my coffin. I was both shocked and offended for a split second. However, I soon realized that she had reawakened me to think about what else was possible in my life. Soon afterwards, I began to get that familiar feeling that I could do more with my life, and just like that, my life began to change. I started to think of ways I could be of service in the world while still being able to be there for my son. Once I convinced myself that pursuing a new business did not mean that I was a bad mother but might help me become a better one, I let go of the fear and fully embraced the new season in our lives.

Why I Wrote This Book

I've wanted to write this book for more than twenty years. The first time I attempted it, I was sitting at Darling Harbour, Sydney on a sunny morning, having breakfast alone while I enjoyed one of my favorite pastimes, people watching. I was merely a transient onlooker, enjoying one of the benefits of being part of the cabin crew to the world's favorite airline, British Airways. As the early morning city workers in their sharp suits ordered lattes and avocado toast or banana bread, I contemplated my life. It was complex. I was finding it difficult to feel free. I was in a loving relationship, but my fiancé had been previously married with two young children, and I wasn't sure if I could cope with what that might bring. As the sounds of a city ready for a new day filled the air, my mind was filled with the idea that I needed to consider my future life deeply. On reflection, it was like an intuitive hit forewarning me of the ups and downs I would encounter and the person I would need to become if I wanted to prove what I truly believed, that love conquers all and that everything works out perfectly in the end.

God knows how much I have put off the actual writing of this book. The self-imposed responsibility to share an honest account of my journey towards inner freedom has left me feeling vulnerable and defeated at times. Doubt about my ability to complete the book coupled with the sheer terror of writing something that might hold no benefit to you, the reader, has kept me awake at night, and I have archived thousands of words that seemed too unhelpful to share.

I make reference to the inner voice a lot in this book. However, another voice is less reliable but often gets the most attention. It's that of the inner critic, or saboteur, who pretends to be our ally. For anyone who has written a book, first let me say, well done. You will know it takes courage to bare your soul and defend the impulse to quit over and over as the voice from the in-house party pooper cautions you that you're wasting your time, that no one cares what you have to say. And the winner every time, which I have no doubt we are all familiar with, is, "Who do you think you are?" In my case, these thoughts are followed by the reminder that I don't have a third-level education and, therefore, have very little credibility.

Ireland is known as the land of saints and scholars. For the record, I am neither. I can't expand on some of what I'm discussing in this book as an academic scholar or theologian. Still, I can share from my experiences as an ordinary woman who loves learning about the truth of who we are and how we must love all parts of ourselves and express our uniqueness for however long we are on this earthly plane.

My wish and intention behind writing this book are to help you find some comfort from your life's ups and downs and to help you remember to *listen to your inner voice, trust its wisdom*, and *know that you are constantly being guided* by a loving energy that sees you as perfect. So, never ever give up on yourself, because you are perfection at your core, and doing the *inner work* allows you to discover that truth for yourself. Only you can do your inner work. You alone have to make those intuitive choices. You have to consciously raise your awareness and trust your instinctual feelings to ultimately trust yourself. Life is all about learning to be responsible for handling every situation that happens to you while you manifest your deepest desires without guilt or shame from the past. This process calls for understanding, patience, and perseverance.

Coming from a deep-rooted belief that we are *one*—we are the same but with different disguises and are so much more than what we see in the mirror. I trust you can see yourself in my story and perhaps adopt some of the practices that have allowed me to return to a state of peace, balance, and ultimate loyalty to my soul.

I know your time is precious, and I truly appreciate you spending some of it with me. So, please read on as I will take you on a journey now from the very beginning.

CHAPTER 1

THE VERY BEGINNING

*The two most important days in your life are the day
you are born and the day you find out why.*

—Anonymous

On a frosty Friday evening in October 1964, my grandmother and her friend marched my mother to the nearby Rotunda Hospital, Dublin, after making her clean windows and scrub floors earlier that day to work through the labor pains. My grandmother, or *Nanny* as we called her, was an old-school midwife with many gifts of healing, and her advice was taken without question. They left my mother at the entrance of the hospital, and as she nervously looked back, my Nanny said with a reassuring wave of her hand, "Off you go! Your baby girl will be born very soon." And I entered the world at 1:50 a.m. on Saturday, October 10.

I am of the baby boomer generation, albeit at the tail end. My birthdate makes me a Libran astrologically and a Dragon according to the Chinese zodiac—which, ahem, a few people would agree with! According to the nursery rhyme "Monday's Child," Saturday's child works hard for a living, and I can confirm that this is absolutely true in my case. However, I'm learning at the time of writing this to embrace the concept that success is not about working hard. It's about doing less and accomplishing more, as decreed by the law of least effort. In numerology, my life path is number 4, which can also be viewed as the master number 22. This suggests that I am devoted and dedicated to being a loyal soul of the light but can be stubborn and prone to procrastination. Thankfully, I engage in personal development each day, which continues to help me get better at the latter. A great fear of mine is not honoring my soul's assignment; however, I push through this fear, and my greatest joy is ensuring this does not become a self-fulfilling prophecy.

I'm the eldest of six children. I have four brothers and one sister. My sister and I are the bookends of our family. My earliest memory was of me falling to the ground in my grandparents' living room, where our adorable dog, Trixie, lunged between my toddler self and a blazing fire to save me from being burned. She suffered minor burns to her coat but was hailed a hero and has always held a special place in my heart.

My Mam and Dad

My mother is one of the most selfless and generous humans I know. She is the person who taught me kindness. I saw her share bowls of sugar and loaves of bread with less fortunate neighbors and comfort many in their times of sorrow and distress. Such was my mother's nature that she was the first person many of our neighbors sought out for advice or assistance in a calamity or when one of the women went into labor in the middle of the night. Her claim to fame was being hands-on during the delivery of several babies in the bedrooms and on the living room floors of our neighbors' homes, thanks to the times she had accompanied her midwife mother.

My mother was born in 1938 in Summerhill, Dublin, the third child of six and the only daughter amongst her five brothers, and was a real daddy's girl. At the age of sixteen, she went to work as a silver service waitress at the headquarters of *An Garda Síochána*, Ireland's police service in the Phoenix Park, where she remained until she got married a little over eight years later.

Without any higher education, she raised six children to live by the codes of "always do your best" and "what's for you will never pass you by." Right or wrong, she always put her children first. While I admire and am grateful for her devotion to her children, as a parent myself living in very different times, I've learned that it's essential to make sure my needs are being met too, a concept that would be utterly foreign to my mother.

I certainly believe that my mother could have achieved so much more had she been made aware of her capabilities and opportunities. I often think about the suppressed women of her generation, and any glimpse of doing something outside of the norm was immediately frowned upon. Her insistence that we would "do better" than her in life suggests that she had some unfulfilled wishes and dreams.

However, whenever I would ask her about what she wanted, she always gave me the same answer: she was happy with what she had, and provided her family was safe and well, that was enough. She led a simple life with some tough times and many losses but has always remained a pillar of strength and support. It says something special when my friends have treated my mother as a friend. I know I have been truly blessed, and I'm so glad that we've had ample time to celebrate and spoil her for her love and devotion to our family.

In contrast, my dad was born in 1936 in rural Ireland, in a picturesque village called Lettermullen, Connemara, Galway. The locals often refer to this part of Ireland as "the next stop is Boston," especially because many relatives left our shores over the past couple of centuries searching for the land of opportunities. Dad was the fourth of eleven children. Described by himself as wild and unruly with a passion for athletics, he ran the roads and beaches with his dog, Prince. At fourteen, he went to a boarding school, where his love of running continued as he competed in events for many years to come.

At eighteen, he joined the Irish Army and, shortly afterwards, *An Garda Síochána*, where he met my mother, a young, shy beauty from Dublin working in the officers' canteen. I love my father's frequent romantic recounting of their courtship. As he reminisces, my mother shrugs and rolls her eyes before she smiles, still somewhat shy and reserved even after 59 years of marriage. Dad joined the prison service in 1961 and remained there until he retired.

He encouraged us as children to enjoy athletics and would train the local community to compete in national competitions. I was horrified when my dad insisted that I compete in the shot put event in the community games. I trained reluctantly and was self-conscious because I equated the event with big, heavy women, and at fifteen, I felt I must have been in that category. I won, but it was bittersweet. I wanted to win in the running, and I often did, but the shot put was not an event I wanted to rave about. I admit to being mortified about it; however, my dad was very proud and full of "I knew you could do this" and "I told you so"s.

My most cherished times with my dad were when we listened to the great musical artists of the 40s and 50s, particularly Mario Lanza. We both loved the old Hollywood movies, and *Carousel* and *Calamity Jane* were among our favorites. It was during those moments that I got to see the tender and sensitive side of my dad. Tears flowed down his cheeks as he became nostalgic and sentimental. Tears fell too when he laughed at the Marx Brothers, Laurel and Hardy, Danny Kaye, and Norman Wisdom. The more offensive humor and entertainment of my youth were never welcome in our home or on our TV screen. Looking back, I do not argue with that, even though it was frustrating at the time. As a parent myself in much more liberal times, I know how both my parents felt because now I try to protect my son from the more unsavory side of life.

Seeing my dad's sentimental side has always been a gift, and I cherish those memories. He has never been shy about his emotions, even though men of his generation didn't openly cry. They had been trained to be stoic, strong, unemotional. Any emotion besides anger was a sign of weakness.

Family Values

In my world, growing up in 1970s' Ireland, much love abounded within the walls of our family home. Love was silent, unspoken, yet known, demonstrated with wholesome meals, clean school uniforms, and concerns about our homework completion. Sunday clothes hung proudly the night before above the polished shoes we had delighted in buying as we were marched like the Von Trapps into Connolly's shoe store in Phibsborough to be professionally fitted and kitted.

A robust moral code that has served me well to this day was enforced in our home and has been fundamental in the rearing of my son. The message was simple: "Always do your best, live as an honest and decent human being, and treat others as you'd like to be treated."

Our Neighbor, Mountjoy Jail

My home lay on the other side of the prison walls of Mountjoy Jail. While some of you grew up surrounded by green fields and rolling hills or the deep blue sea, I grew up in a concrete jungle with a major hospital to my left, a prison to my right, and a busy road in between where I'd hear the sounds of the cattle being herded to the mart and market during the early hours of the morning while the sirens of the emergency services seemed to fill the air for the remainder of the day.

Our home was part of a community of families where every man was a prison officer. People could relate to one another because of their shared occupation, which created a great kinship. While criminals and prisoners are not in everyone's everyday experience, I grew up in close proximity to them.

Whenever our home was being decorated, both the prison officer and prisoners carried out the task. This was where I witnessed my mother's show of equality as she welcomed many a prisoner to our table to eat with us and treated them with dignity. I do not doubt that this kind of exposure has influenced my empathetic interactions with people because I understand that "there but for the grace of God, go I."

Global Citizen

As a child, encouraged by aunts, uncles, and grandparents, I would stand on the sofa using a sweeping brush handle as a microphone and belt out "All Kinds of Everything," as if I were performing in the Eurovision Song Contest myself, to rapturous applause from the very biased smiling and enthusiastic audience.

A dream of being on a stage in front of people was born. I enjoyed making people happy. I wanted to spread joy and hope to many people everywhere, but I did not believe that a girl from Dublin 7 would ever have that opportunity. How ridiculous it made me feel even to contemplate this notion, and it remained my secret dream for five decades. On reflection, I can see how that dream could easily have remained a dream. I had very little self-belief despite having so much desire. What I had in my mind was not anything I could have discussed with a career guidance teacher. I'm not sure if I really knew precisely what I wanted to do. The evidence was in my heart all along as to what I was born to do; it just took a while for it to reveal itself fully and for me to have the confidence to own it.

Inequality and injustice went against the characteristics of the Libran nature I possess, where fairness and a strong sense of justice are paramount. I wanted so badly to be a global citizen, meaning I wanted just to be me, accepted for who I was, and able to love and accept others as they were, wherever they were. Of course, I didn't have that language back then, but I knew I would have friends from all over the world, from every creed and cultural background, with diverse upbringings, and I wanted to feel equal to them. As a wise friend said to me recently, we are educated to be individuals, separate from God and one another, when in actuality, we are all connected and interdependent. We need one another. This individualistic mentality creates only division and disharmony among us. It leads to rivalry, opposition, control, and manipulation. I seemed to know this from a very young age. Considering the world today, if ever there were a need for people to come together as one, it is now.

At 13, I got my first job motivated by a school trip to Italy and the awareness that my parents couldn't afford to let me go. Purposefully, I decided to take it into my own hands to earn the money. So began the realization of my dream of exploring new places and the start of much globe-trotting. The flower shop on the corner near the Mater Hospital in Dublin became another source of education, where I learned everything from arranging bouquets to stocktaking and customer service skills. I can still recall getting my first wage and the satisfaction of having money I'd earned in my pocket. The best part was that I never asked my parents again for a penny, buying whatever I needed and loving my independence.

There was a great mix of customers to this busy corner store, from the locals to visitors to the hospital and staff. One man, in particular, stood out and held a special place in my heart. His name was Walter, from County Kerry. He'd call in most days and stand around for several hours chatting. I'm sure it was a welcome break from what must have been a lonely life. Walter was wise and offered sage advice at times about world affairs and living a purposeful life to whoever would listen. I liked to talk to him about some of my dreams. He never judged me or made me feel foolish but instead encouraged me to pursue them. He probably never knew how much I regarded him, but here I am, acknowledging his input into my young life. Sometimes, it takes just one person to give you hope.

Forged by Fire

I'll never forget the fatal Stardust nightclub fire. It was Valentine's night in 1981 when I had finished my shift at the shop. In keeping with my desire to sample the whole wide world, I was excited to taste my first-ever Indian curry. It was fiery hot, possibly foreshadowing later events. We remember some of the most trivial details when an event has an emotional impact, such as the tragedy on that fateful night. It was close to midnight, and I was enjoying a chat with my mother and her friend, debating whether I liked this new cuisine or not, when a loud knocking on our front door alerted us to an emergency across the road in the hospital. Without hesitation, we ran over to see how we could help. That was when one of the staff recognized me from the shop where I worked, handed me a clipboard and pen, and told me to register the patients as they were being admitted. I didn't think twice about it, and truth be told, I knew I was meant to be there.

That day, I left at midday, and to say I was traumatized was an understatement. The smell of burning flesh and hair was hard to shake off, and the sight and sounds of screaming victims left me unnerved for a long time. The memory of offering hope to a father who was frantically searching for his son haunted me the most. I remember saying that his name was familiar, but I couldn't find him on the register. People were coming and going. There was sheer hysteria from all angles, patients in distress and pain, the staff running off their feet with insufficient supplies for an emergency of this nature, and the victims' relatives screaming while trying to locate their loved ones. Terrified parents grabbed my arms, begging me to tell them that their loved one was safe and being treated somewhere in the hospital. Several people had asked me about this particular young man, and I thought I had admitted him in my confusion. It later transpired that his son was one of the victims identified in the nightclub. It was like a bad movie, and I had nightmares for months afterwards and prayed fervently for forgiveness for my mistake. It had been mayhem, with three people lying on a bed, and some of them next to a corpse.

I managed to create some meaning out of this horrific event. On that tragic night, I discovered that I was able to cope quite well in a crisis. I was recognized shortly afterwards with a handwritten letter from the head sister on duty commending me for my assistance and sense of responsibility. I was just sixteen years old and knew for sure that I wanted to help and make a difference in the world. Little did I know how many twists and turns that desire would take.

~

CHAPTER 2

WE ARE ALL EXPRESSIONS OF GOD

*Awakening is not changing who you are
but discarding who you are not.*

—Deepak Chopra

My God and the Catholic God

Reflecting on my childhood, I see the home where I grew up, a happy home for the most part, although I can't help but feel the confusion that consumed me around God for many of my formative years and the frustration at not being able to speak about it. I used to play with my brother, pray with my father, and jump on my bed while singing at the top of my lungs, but I often remember times when I would cry nervously at night at the top of the stairs, not wanting my mother to visit her parents in case something were to happen to her.

Our avenue was always busy. The neighbors were friends, and all the children played for hours on the road under the watchful eye of one or more of the mothers or older children. Our favorite pastime was playing hopscotch on our chalked out "piggy beds" as we kicked a tin of shoe polish from square to square while hopping on one foot. My next favorite pastime was kiss chasing with the boys. It was harmless, but I was a hopeless romantic even as a child.

Over the years, as I became more interested in spiritual development, I craved to remember what my inner child knew all those years ago. I've thought about how much I'd love the chance to speak to the younger me and ask her what she knew about life and God. So, I did the next best thing: I'd hold an old photo of myself in my hand and look into my eyes, trying to get inside my six-year-old head to find out exactly what I was thinking and what I knew about the mystery of life back then. I'd ask the child in the photo, "Who are you? What were you born to do? What do you know? What have I forgotten?" The answers come; they're always the same. I'm told that I am love and that I'm here to share the message of love. I'm also told to be patient and wait, that the truth will always reveal itself. This doesn't mean that I've always been in the love vibe throughout my life, because I haven't, but I'm grateful to have been able to accept many of my challenges and tormentors through my spiritual development. Being willing to see others and situations through the eyes of love is not only liberating for our spirit but aids us in transcending a victim mentality, which is destructive and disempowering.

As I looked back, part of me wanted to relive some of the scenes so I could edit them and replace them with what I'd like to have happened. Mostly, I wished I had been able to say aloud how much I believed that God was being done a disservice and that we had it all wrong. We were not *separate* from God—but *were* God.

As I got older, the inner rebel surfaced. I became more vocal in expressing my thoughts and feelings, which invariably ended in arguments with my father. His intentions were always well meaning. He grew up when following the commandments of the Catholic Church was unquestioned and formed the basis of many facets of life. It seemed at this time that the notion of ever questioning the status quo was not even a consideration. It was a case of accepting and getting on with it.

I, on the other hand, had questions, and lots of them. The thoughts I never spoke openly about until I was a teenager reflected what I still believe to this day—that we are all expressions of God and that we had done God an injustice. I withheld my interrogation out of fear of rejection, mainly because I felt terrible for being so defiant. I never wanted to hurt my father. For the sheer irreverence of such thoughts, I imagined I would be met with accusations of blasphemy and be burned at the stake as a modern-day witch. When I did start talking about my thoughts on the subject, even friends who loved me often spoke about me as being "a bit out there." I was often called a witch and a tree hugger, neither of which upset me. In fact, I enjoyed it.

My father delighted in my positive responses to the many relics he brought into our home and my fascination with the stories of the children in Garabandal and Fatima who claimed to have had several apparitions from Our Lady. I believed in the power of such things, although I disliked the underlying threat that the world would come to an end if we did not pray and repent. You can imagine how I saw my fate unfold, given my reluctance to participate in such devotions.

Whatever anyone else thought of me, I felt trapped in my head and heart and thought I would implode; such was the pain and confusion I felt deep within. I was a hormonal, frustrated teenager with no one to talk to about my internal conflicts and was starting to believe that I needed to move far away. This was an isolating time for me. However, I have found from working with clients that self-discovery can often be lonely.

I always felt that being guilty until proven innocent was the underlying ethos of my religion, which saw me as a sinner first. It always felt wrong to me, but still, the power of negativity prevailed, leaving me feeling like my very existence was tainted. So as adults, it's tough for many Catholics, in particular, to believe that any part of us is perfect when the foundation of our belief system is to confess our wrongdoings, failings, and misdemeanors—to say that we are sinners. It left me feeling sad, withdrawn, and at a loss.

The irony of the weekly Saturday morning confession was that I lied most weeks. It was essential to be clean and tidy with our list of "sins" committed to memory, primed for the telling. I tried to think of what I would say to the priest, especially if I'd been a "good girl" since my last confession, just seven days earlier. I'd think, "This is absolutely nuts! I have to make stuff up so that I can sit in a confessional box and tell the priest that I am a bad girl because I was cheeky to my mother?" (Now, sometimes that was true.) What I am confessing to you now was that I sometimes told the priest lies to be pardoned, and I practiced them over and over in my head, like I was memorizing my times tables for math, on my way to the church and while I sat in the pews awaiting my turn. The best part about the experience was coyly waving at my friends, who were also there under similar duress, seeking to regain the grace of God lost by sin and wrongdoings. From the looks on their faces, I doubt I was the only one questioning the soundness of this religious sacrament.

Mainly, I was lying to honor the weekly ritual intended to absolve my misgivings. I was supposed to feel better for having done this, but in reality, it made me feel despondent and disconnected.

Confusion and Questions

The root of my confusion was that mentioning love and fear in the same sentence seemed absurd. I never understood how they could coexist when describing God. I distinctly remember being told that God was love but that he was also a judge who would send me to the fires of hell for my sins if I misbehaved.

Being threatened that my life would end in an inferno confused me. On the one hand, it scared me, and on the other hand, I was sure that this was not the God I knew inside. I can recall a feeling, or perhaps it's better described as an inner knowing, that the people I knew and loved had God all wrong. To me, God was invisible yet present and filled me with a never-ending supply of love. He (I would like to clarify that I don't think of God as male necessarily, but for the book, I am referring to God in the masculine) made me feel with an unshakable certainty that one day I would be free to explain this awareness I had developed at such a young age.

Questions flooded my mind frequently, such as . . .

"How can God love me and judge me at the same time?"

"How can God be scary and loving all at once?"

"Why am I a Catholic? Why not a Jew? Jesus was a Jew."

"Who made religion? Is it the truth? How do you know it's the truth?"

"Who wrote the Bible? Is it accurate?" (Adding, "I heard it's man-made and has been lost in translation.")

"Why are there so many religions if there is only *one* God, as I'm told?"

"What about the people I want to meet from all around the world from different backgrounds, with different skin colors and religions? Can I not share my life with them?"

"Are we superior as Catholics? Is everyone else inferior? How does that work?"

"Who says that you need to be a Catholic to be in the front row with God?"

"Am I allowed to speak to people who are different from me?"

"Am I going to heaven or hell, and where is either?"

"Why do people kill one another in the name of God?"

I always had questions, but many external answers were not in harmony with those I felt within. The one thing my dad told me that resonated with me most was that I was born to serve God. I was put on Earth to do something, and if I prayed to God and asked what that was, I would be answered. I loved and believed this idea, later discovering from Deepak Chopra that it is indeed true.

Our lovely family friend, a Jesuit priest, was enlisted to aid my dad in persuading me that I was going down a treacherous path with my questioning and challenging manner. I was sixteen years old and was bored to tears of praying in a traditional way. As the three of us sat in our living room by the fire, I proceeded to share my doubts about my religious upbringing and ask questions that neither of them could answer. It left a very concerned father shaking his head in both disappointment and despair at his less-than-obedient daughter and a jolly priest feeling deflated. Looking back, I can see I have always had an investigative nature and how it came to help me in my various jobs, especially in my current work.

My inner rebel was alive and well. Foolishly, I joked with my friends that I had been exorcised and that the dark forces within had been purged. But the idea that I was possessed or impious was no laughing matter, nor was the utter seclusion

I felt at a deep level from holding a contradictory opinion to that of my family and community. It seemed my opinion was unwelcomed, and conformity was the name of the game. I had started to break some rules. Little did I know that I would break much bigger ones later on.

Seeking Answers

Religion did not nourish my soul, and I knew I had to find another way. I've heard that religion is God's politics made by man, and as in politics, it's impossible to get all sides to agree on anything. In the civilized world, we are supposed to have freedom of choice and are entitled to our opinion. However, being forced to form an allegiance with a political party, or in this case, a religion, just because our parents and grandparents had seemed to be in opposition of that free will. I know as children we have no say in such matters; my frustration is that the people around me seemed closed to these questions, and I felt that my alternative thinking and opinions were not allowed.

When *The Celestine Prophecy* was released in 1993, being a seeker, I devoured it as I had started devouring all books just like it. I was living in London, having left my career as a Garda that should have taken me to retirement, and was now talking about all things that fell into the category of New Age consciousness. Once again, I was a massive cause for concern to the people around me and, in particular, my father

Such was his unease that once he visited me in London and invited me to an event in a church where he summoned a priest to my side. He had relayed his concerns about me to this cross-looking priest who, without any hesitation, proceeded to warn me of the inherent danger of getting wrapped up in this unacceptable movement. He told me in the same breath to remove the necklace I was wearing that held an Egyptian ankh, the ancient hieroglyphic symbol of life. This necklace was a gift from my mother. I was furious at his audacity and utter disregard for my side of the story, but in those moments, I remained silent. As I stood there, in a familiar triangle with my father and a priest, I felt as if I were on trial, this time in a church. Filled with mixed emotions from shame to anger, I had a moment of doubt and asked myself, "What if I'm wrong?" I never wanted to hurt my father; I knew he wanted to help me. It certainly would have made my life easier as I would have had rules to follow, and I would be in the majority and not in the isolated minority. Within this questioning, I heard the comforting voice within telling me to be patient and stay in the energy of love, and all would be well.

I continued to wear my much-loved necklace, and I did not stop reading the books that were supporting me in opening my mind and soothing my soul. If anything, being told to denounce some of the things that gave me inner strength and heightened awareness was another example that added to my determination in seeking the truth for myself. Failing to explore the truth seemed like such a betrayal of my soul's mission, and I was adamant that that wouldn't happen. My passion for the truth created a hunger, a yearning for more knowledge. I wanted the truth, and there was no way I was going to starve my spirit.

When the inspirational book *A New Earth* by Eckhart Tolle came under my radar, it profoundly affected me. He writes about sin early in the book. He says *sin* in Greek means "to miss the mark," as an archer misses the target, so *to sin* means "to miss the point of human existence." While many would contradict this definition, in my opinion, I feel that the religious teachers I had met along the way missed the mark entirely, often devaluing humanity when they delivered a doctrine that made people feel immoral, dishonest, and ungodly by virtue of their very existence.

My understanding of how inaccurately we were being educated about God and our true identity was always close to the surface of my being. For a start, we have complicated God, given him many names, and witnessed wars in his name. We've been left feeling confused, and perhaps that's how the authorities want us to feel. A confused mind is a vulnerable mind and is more easily manipulated. We can learn for ourselves and our children to find another way to experience God.

With my Pollyanna hat on and a borrowed magic wand, I would dream of a world of equality and togetherness, not naïve to the complexity of life. If only we could all come together, admit our mistakes, and see one another as a reflection of ourselves. If only we could start over with a new narrative that leads with love and respect for one another and the encouragement to be our authentic Selves without disregarding our fellow travelers. What if we started to tell our children that the purpose of their lives was to find out what they were born to do rather than trying to force them into a box called conformity? What if we understood that love is the energy of creation and can mend more than a broken heart? What if we were told from the beginning that we are spiritual beings in a physical body? Do you think we might be less judgmental and overly critical? What if we were reminded that we are here to unlearn, learn, and remember our magnificence? Do you think that we might be willing to help one another more genuinely? What if we were constantly reminded that we are unique with innate gifts and talents? Do you think there would be less bullying? And what if we were told that we will make many mistakes but that it's okay to do so, and that is how we learn? Do you think we might be inclined to apologize, forgive, strive, reach higher, and give life more of a go? Or how about knowing that living a full, abundant life is our birthright? Do you think we might be braver and kinder?

I know that's the kind of world I want to live in.

The goal of all goals is to be happy and at peace within ourselves. Responding to life's tests in the most loving and compassionate way whilst looking for the good in every challenge and freely speaking our truth sees to that goal being fulfilled. That, to me, is heaven on earth.

Another Way

Whilst continuing my quest for understanding the meaning of life in April of 2008, I had the great fortune to attend a talk in Dublin by Deepak Chopra, a teacher who had had a profound impact on my life since I'd first been introduced to his work in my twenties. The first time I played the old cassette I'd been given and heard his voice and the words he was saying, I was hooked. He spoke directly to my truth-starved soul in a way that I had been searching for the longest time.

His message made me feel more alive than I had ever felt. I had a new perspective, yet it felt familiar; I recognized the truth when I heard it. He helped me to let go of the self-imposed label of the rebel, the disobedient girl, as I had often felt when I was growing up. His words of wisdom allowed me to breathe again, dream again, and tap into the recesses of my soul. The more he shared, the more I remembered what I felt as a child. His references to the idea that *we are one* felt soothing to my soul. We are the same; we come from the same source, a force of energy, and we have the same needs. Fascinated by the mystical and the invisible, I always felt that this idea was true. Of course, I couldn't prove it scientifically, but for me, the evidence lay in how it made me feel. There was an inner knowing, like flashbacks to something I understood that needed no clarification. I couldn't explain it, but I believed I had found the truth, and I was captivated.

At the event in the National Concert Hall in Dublin, it was announced that Deepak and his team from the Chopra Center in California were coming to Ireland in July to host their signature retreat, the Seduction of Spirit. My inner voice was on full volume, telling me persuasively, like an eager child, "Go! You have to be there. This is going to be transformational for you." So, I presented my credit card and signed up for one of the most cathartic experiences of my life.

It wasn't easy for me to leave my son for a whole week, especially since I had not left him for more than a couple of hours previously, but I knew that I had to go. My mother would take good care of him, and we would all benefit from this experience. Also, behind my decision to go was an overwhelming desire to learn something that would help me be the best parent I could be. I wanted my son to grow up with an open mind and heart, to have an awareness of what mattered, and to be kind and accepting of the people in front of him. I wanted him to feel free to find his path and purpose in life and to know that his main goal was to do something in life that he loved.

Once again, my inner voice was leading me to where I was meant to be, and the more I trusted going with the flow, the more aligned it became. Attending the retreat was one of the best decisions I've ever made. I was transported to what I can describe only as heaven for seven glorious days. Surrounded by 560 people from all over the world, I felt so connected to everyone around me and loved every second of this magical experience. My dream for so many years of being in the presence of this great teacher had finally come true— another manifestation materialized.

One of the rituals at the Seduction of Spirit retreat was to be gifted with our primordial sound mantra. I was so excited to receive my mantra based on my date, time, and place of birth. An English translation of *mantra* is "mind instrument." It is a tool to help during meditation when you become aware that your mind has drifted to thoughts or emotions and sounds in the environment. As you silently repeat your mantra, it allows you to enter into an expanded state of awareness, experiencing more profound levels of peace and possibility. What I loved most about this practice was how it reminded me of my soul's mission and to trust in its unfoldment.

The highlight of the retreat for me was the yoga classes. I indulged myself in these heart-opening practices every morning before breakfast and again in the evening before dinner. I attended every one of them. Even though I'd been to random classes here and there worldwide, nothing felt as good as these particular classes. I was obsessed in the healthiest possible way. So, when they announced that we could train with Deepak Chopra in both yoga and meditation, I knew I had to sign up.

I saw why it was so important to have left my son for a whole week; here it was right before me, the next rung on the ladder of my purpose, my path. I had fallen in love with this way of living, but only one problem remained: I did not see myself as a yoga teacher. I felt more like a sumo wrestler than a svelte yoga teacher, and it didn't help to see so much evidence of how I thought a yoga teacher should look from the gorgeous goddesses of the Chopra squad.

Thankfully, a sincere and nervous conversation with one such goddess culminated with me signing up. She made me feel that I was worthy of teaching yoga, and while neither of us addressed that it was my vain ego making all the noise, I knew that yoga and meditation were the right paths for me to follow, and my ego was just going to have to get used to it. Moving forward with this decision felt so right and easy, and so began a journey that has lifted me to new levels of awareness and joy ever since. I had discovered another way to work in the world with no more institutional restrictions on me. It took me a while longer to realize I had become an entrepreneur and that this was only the beginning.

I never doubted the constancy of how this approach to living an integrous life made me feel, in contrast with my religious upbringing. They were poles apart in terms of the levels of joy and freedom I felt. Truth and trust conjoined in the most revolutionary way. I had come home to myself and would never again allow myself to feel wrong for listening to my internal guidance system and following this enlightening path.

During the retreat, we participated in daily meditations. At first, it was challenging to sit still and not feel agitated or curious about what everyone else was doing. However, the meditation habit was forming, and the promises of feeling relaxed and at peace were fulfilled. Deepak guided us to explore our soul by asking significant questions, one of which was, "*Who am I?*" During one such inquiry, I remembered a message I received as a child when I was saying the family rosary reluctantly.

I was immediately transported back to my childhood home when I was six years old, dutifully kneeling beside my mother. At the same time, my younger brother played on the floor, and my father led us through our daily rosary. At that moment, I recalled the whisper I received in my right ear, "*There is another way.*" It was as if I were hearing it for the first time, except this time, I had a greater understanding of what those words meant.

"There is another way. . . ." I said the words over and over, followed by, "Of course, there is another way; there's always another way." Everything was beginning to make sense.

Suddenly, given my environment, the most significant meaning of this message was revealed to me: *there is another way to know God.* It later came to have many more connotations in other areas of life. It was so easy to know God, and the moment I realized this was critical for my life and the meaning of my soul's purpose. It wasn't unusual to hear sniffles and crying during this weeklong dive into the depths of our spirit, and I broke the silence right then and there as I seemed unable to control the years of tears I had bottled up inside as they flowed down my face and into my lap. It was both exhilarating and intimidating simultaneously—exhilarating because I knew I had touched upon a truth and intimidating because I felt that I would someday have to share this truth, which was daunting.

You could say that my inner voice had accomplished its mission in guiding me to this pivotal moment. At this moment, a truth I had long known but forgotten was exposed to me. Just as the name of the retreat suggested, my spirit was entirely seduced, my heart was cracked open, and my soul was ablaze. I certainly got my money's worth at this retreat, especially when reflecting on my past experiences. I had withdrawn from everyday life. It wasn't quite the cave in the Himalayas. Still, this hotel in south Dublin became a sanctuary where I felt nourished and protected, surrounded by fellow seekers, led by a truth teacher who brought timeless, ancient wisdom to the modern world. The experience presented me with an opportunity to reflect on my life. I was able to finally forgive myself for breaking one of the ten commandments by marrying my divorced husband and bearing the humiliation of feeling like an adulterer. I could banish any shame I felt around my beliefs about religion and the subsequent disagreements with my family. No anger, blame, or guilt remained, only an understanding and appreciation of the opportunities that my life had presented me with and the most potent, overwhelming awareness of love.

Something had shifted. I was vulnerable, yet I felt liberated. My inner voice was clear as it reminded me of my power to make whatever came my way all right. I had a newfound faith and felt pardoned for any wrongdoing, which included my lack of confidence in expressing more lovingly what I knew to be true for so many years.

I now have confidence in saying that God spoke to me when I was six years old. He has spoken to me all my life, even though at times, I wasn't listening. Sometimes, his guidance would come through a book, an angel card, a stranger at a bus stop, a teacher, or a child. I am so open to acting with complete trust and conviction upon the messages I receive. Being able to trust and have faith in this guidance has helped me to accept and respect my father's religious views, to never give up on becoming a mother, to change careers despite concern and objections from my nearest and dearest, and a whole host of other choices, including marrying my husband and following my heart. This trust has helped to turn a naturally impatient person into a more tolerant and understanding one.

That message has taken on so much more meaning as I reflect on my life over the past fifty years. My six-year-old self didn't have a voice or language to express her distress and be heard. My opinion wasn't welcome. "Children should be seen and not heard" was the rule, as I am sure many readers have also experienced. I had to respect my father and swallow my feelings about religion, but God heard my silent interrogation and answered me. He whispered in my ear, "There is another way." At that time, it meant that there was another way to know God, but it has also come to highlight in my life that there is another way to get married, parent, do meaningful work, and find solutions to life's problems by being willing to look at things differently. This message is the foundation of creating miracles, seeing things differently, and not be rigidly attached to anything. It invites us to be open to solving our problems by seeking a spiritual solution.

I'm not trying to influence you to believe in what I believe in. I'm not criticizing my parents, teachers, priests, or politicians for their part in my education and upbringing and how they influenced me. I am not an expert in theology or religious studies, and I'm not condemning anyone for their beliefs. We're all on a journey, and I believe we each awaken in our own time. We are all operating at different levels of awareness. Something usually happens to wake us up. For many, this level of awareness follows a tragedy and loss or maybe a decision to find the answers to the relentless rhetorical questioning, "Is this it? Is this all there is for me? Surely there's got to be more." What I know for sure is to remain open and curious and allow yourself to explore the possibilities for your life and evolve into your greatness.

CHAPTER 3

~

LET LOVE LEAD

*Love recognizes no barriers. It jumps hurdles, leaps
fences, penetrates walls to arrive at its destination
full of hope.*

—Maya Angelou

Love: The Constant Whisper in My Soul

The one thing above all else that has been crucial for me is remaining close to my family. As I've discovered in a family of eight, differences exist in personalities and viewpoints. Many families are a good representation of humanity at large, and you might learn all you need to know about the human race at your kitchen table.

My dad and I never truly fell out, not even when he wrote me a long letter of concern when I was training with the Chopra Center, fearing I may have joined a cult. Our relationship was solid. I knew how to work around the conversations to avoid a falling out. My intention was always to allow love to lead the way and see things from his point of view, even when I vehemently disagreed with something. I respected him even when I didn't feel heard. I love him with all my heart.

However, as a teen, if I'd been allowed to watch *Dallas* and figure out who shot J.R., it would have brought our relationship back then to a whole new level. Such viewing was regarded as unsuitable, but thanks to my more lenient mother, I got to see the show occasionally when dad was working late. It was our little secret and one that solidified our friendship.

Dad has no time for trivia or nonsense, and as I got older, I became the same. Don't get me wrong, I absolutely love to have a laugh, but I always feel that everything I do has to have a purpose. One of our favorite things to do together was to go running. I especially loved our runs up and down the sand dunes at the beach in Donabate and around the Furry Glen in the Phoenix Park. As an enthusiastic runner, my dad was hard to beat in the many military-type drills he set for me, no doubt a discipline he'd gained from his brief time in the army. I loved those times we spent together and will cherish them forever.

The conversations between the sprints and jumping jacks were always encouraging but invariably infused with a reminder to obey the commandments and pray for salvation. Sometimes, I pretended not to hear what felt heavy and bubble-bursting to this young and enthusiastic teen. I wished my dad could just talk about athletics and music; I wished religion was not a part of our lives. Even though I'm sure the members of many households grew up in similar circumstances, it seemed that none of my friends had the same level of exposure. I wanted to scream at times to get my father just to enjoy the moment, the time together, and the natural, loving energy between us. It became a thorn in my side and a trigger, but because I didn't want it to come between us, I had to dig deep to rise above the frustration and let my love and acceptance smooth out our differences.

There always seemed to be whispers of support guiding me throughout my youth, especially when I felt conflicted. It was as if they were directing me to have faith in myself, which led me to expect that everything would work out all right, no matter what. The constant message has always been to *let love lead, just love.* And so, I never screamed but chose to trust that someday we would mutually respect one another's choices.

I remember having an interesting healing session with a therapist who rented a room in my holistic healing center just a few years ago. He picked up from my energy that I had been parenting my parents since my early years, apparently assuming the role to lead the way for my siblings and break some of our familial patterns. I've often been referred to as the third parent to my brothers and sister. Much as I can identify with some of that, I occasionally would look at my dad with compassion, never wanting it to turn to pity as that would have been an insult to a man who was doing his utmost. However, what I was muttering under my breath was never spoken aloud: "Oh Dad, please relax. We're all going to be okay. The truth will be revealed, and you don't need to save our souls. That's not your responsibility."

"I Want to Hear 'I Love You'"

When I was about eight or nine, I was walking to school with my mother and younger brother. It was a typical morning, except on this occasion, I looked up at my mother while holding her hand and asked her if we, as a family, could say that we loved each other. I said, "I want to hear the words 'I love you.'"

There was an awkwardness to me posing the question and more so in my mother's response. I took her unawares, and I know now that she was shy, but it also seems those three words have not been very familiar language throughout generations of families.

It wasn't that I didn't feel love or was unloved, but I wanted what I saw and heard on TV shows such as *The Waltons, The Brady Bunch*, and especially *Little House on the Prairie*. I was fascinated with the characters' lives and torn between wanting to be like Laura Ingalls or Marcia Brady. But mostly, I wanted the "I love you"s that they had. I was still too naïve to understand the difference between acting and reality and certainly too unaware of the emptiness that those three words held for many who said them often. However, I pride myself on following my heart in breaking the mold, one of many, and perfecting the ease with which I can say those words authentically.

I promised myself years ago to let my children know how much I loved them when I became a mother. So, Finn was lathered in love, and it felt so good to raise him with such a powerful emotion without any shyness or fear. I'm glad I soaked up his affection during those years when I could hold him close. Now that he's a teenager, my affection is less welcome, but I persist with the "I love you"s and hugs, even though I might get a grunt or an impatient shrug before it's back to the gaming and banter with the pals online. There's nothing quite like a spontaneous bear hug and smile when he extends them. I'm always willing to receive and grateful to hear him express his love freely.

Sadly, too many of us have never felt or been told that we were loved, leaving us searching for the love we never got in all the wrong places, such as through addiction, abusive relationships, and other pitfalls, as they often replace the unworthiness and rejection that consume us. I've seen it with many clients in my work as a clinical hypnotherapist and coach, but I also witnessed it as a Garda with both colleagues and lawbreakers. Thankfully, people can find solutions to these emotional issues when they take back control of their minds and connect with their nonphysical Self, their spirit. A new narrative around self-love has developed in more recent years that invites more of us to awaken to the power of loving ourselves no matter what. The old idea that self-love is egocentric and selfish is being replaced by the new concept of authentic, unconditional love for ourselves. Self-love is a modern-day panacea available to us all to heal the emptiness from neglect and an unfounded belief that what you have to say and who you are don't matter. An unlearning is called for around this concept because we have to delete the old conditioning and programming that has left us feeling bereft of our beautiful, loving essence and replace it moment by moment with new suggestions that we are both worthy and deserving of all that we want.

Love is the answer always; it will always find a way. Why are so many of us afraid to speak its language? We make it conditional, just like our happiness. It becomes something we get as a result of something else. For example, we say we'll be happy when we find the right partner, and then when we do, we create conditions that make it difficult for our partner to love us. Worse, we often place the responsibility for our happiness and sense of worth on our partners. Have you experienced this? Well, I have. I didn't know anything about self-love. I've been wrong about a few things in my life, such as the belief I held that it wasn't a good night out unless I got drunk when I was younger. This makes me cringe today. I also believed that a successful relationship was based on each person lavishing love on the other, putting the other's needs before their own. Whenever this intensity wasn't reciprocated, I felt unlovable, unattractive, and undesirable. How we undervalue ourselves!

We must learn to love ourselves first and then teach people how to treat us. This requires us to know who we are and believe in our worth. A cousin to self-love is self-praise, and we now know that it is the cure to another more unwelcome cousin, self-criticism. Like most people, you will be pretty good at criticizing yourself and not so good at praising yourself. Maybe you heard that old saying, "self-praise is no praise," or you listen to echoes of being called a braggart or a show-off if you ever dared to say something kind about yourself or put yourself forward to do something wild or exciting. Never has it been more critical to spread this message of worthiness and self-love to offset society's harsh criticism and shaming. Learning about the truth of who you are and being ready to embrace that truth can lead you to explore what's possible for your life.

When you start to love and value yourself, others will mirror that behavior back to you. People can love you only to the degree that you love yourself. If you don't love yourself, you may not accept love from someone else or, worse, you may put up with their abuse because they think you're available for that. In other words, you can reject the very love you seek, or you can allow someone to reject you when you don't love yourself. You don't think that you're worthy of another's love and attention. You might even be shocked that someone you like likes you back. Where did all these hang-ups come from? We learned to think and act in this way from what we saw happening around us as children by our parents and carers in the schoolyard and classrooms, molding us into a limited version of ourselves where only a fraction of our potential is expressed.

A pattern of doubting and subsequently denying ourselves becomes the norm, and that can leave us with a closed heart, shutting out the infinite supply of love and happiness that flows from within. Sadly, this translates to an abandonment of our Self and a disconnection from our truth. Except many of us are unaware of this *Self* with a capital S until we get so fed up with being fed up with repeated cycles that bring sadness and anxiety and leave us despondent and frustrated about life that we finally embark on the search for more meaning and inner peace.

We begin to accept that many of our *mentors* have been our tor*mentors*, and with further self-discovery, we can learn to forgive them with love and understanding. Forgiveness is a process but is a vital stepping-stone in liberating us from blame, shame, and victimhood. Forgiveness doesn't mean that we're condoning someone else's behavior, but rather it frees us up from living as a diluted version of ourselves. When we hold a grudge, our energy contracts; it makes us small, and we inadvertently feel powerless, waiting for someone else to fix the problem. The problem with that is you could be left waiting a long time. Now, who's in charge of your future? We can take control of the situation and learn to let go and forgive; otherwise, the person who wronged us will always have a piece of us.

Whether we are forgiving ourselves or someone else, we are activating our heart energy, and that energy is love. We remove the heavy armor and open our hearts to both giving and receiving love. We set ourselves free to create our lives with love.

~

CHAPTER 4

CREATING A LIFE

Be yourself. Everyone else is already taken.

—Oscar Wilde

The Great Escape

Home was noisy, and I was restless. Travel and adventure and my love of the French language fueled my desire to get away. I was ready to flee the nest and prove I could take care of myself. So began a six-month exodus to France as an au pair. The thrill of traveling alone was short-lived after I was robbed by the French woman and her friends who had helped me navigate the then wildly confusing Charles de Gaulle Airport and escorted me to the train station at Gare du Nord in Paris. I was left in utter shock, straddling my luggage, luckily with my train ticket in hand. They stole my handbag, which contained my hard-earned cash, farewell gifts from my distraught family and friends, and my passport, among other things.

Suddenly, my mother's fears were realized, and I felt exposed and unprotected when a stranger came to my aid. Her name was Zeta, and she was Swiss. She took me to the police and reported the crime. She rang the French family I was meeting and explained what had happened to me. Finally, she handed me one hundred francs to get something to eat. I have never forgotten her kindness. She restored my faith in humanity and has been an example I have emulated on occasion since.

As I sat for hours awaiting my train to Brioude, a small town in south-central France in the region known as Auvergne, any regret at my stubbornness in pursuing this life experience was dismissed when I met the wonderful family with whom I would spend six amazing months. So began my love of *pain au chocolat*, baguettes, *fromage*, and French *parfum*. The French lifestyle was worlds apart from the one I'd grown up in, and it made me feel truly free. For starters, I lived in a renovated, old cloisters in a quaint village in the countryside where I walked with the children in my care daily. Sometimes, a snake would wriggle its way across the path in front of us. I was stunned into semi-paralysis the first time it happened, but then I got used to it. I had not just my own bedroom but a whole floor to myself and my very own bathroom. There was so much space. I was particularly drawn to the elegance and sophistication of the lifestyle I was becoming accustomed to.

My time in France was an eye-opening half year of living a privileged life. I'd visited the Prince's Palace of Monaco, the beaches of Nice, and the ski resorts of Chamonix. I was introduced to vintage red wine and champagne and experienced intoxication for the first time. I got charmed by Jean-Paul and had a real French kiss. I was sampling a life I had dreamed of as a child, becoming that global citizen. I discovered how much I loved to experience different cultures, cuisines, and languages. I felt expanded on so many levels and knew I wanted an exciting life of luxury and depth.

All good things must come to an end, and eventually, it was time for me to depart France and say *au revoir* to a life that taught me so much about myself and what I wanted. I considered not going home and moving to Paris, where I'd fall passionately in love and live happily ever after. It must have been George Michael serenading me with "Careless Whisper" every night on *Radio Luxembourg* that ignited my romantic musings.

One day, a letter from my dad arrived to inform me that I'd been called to attend the medical examination and Irish (Gaelic) oral interview to be accepted to train with *An Garda Síochána*. I had six weeks to prepare. Moving to Paris was soon forgotten as I got busy with the business of going home.

The first thing I had to do was tell my lovely French family and assist them in hiring my replacement. Then in a panic, I had to shed the weight I'd gained from over-indulging in the calorific delights of the region so that I would pass the medical examination. The dormant former athlete had to return at speed, and so in addition to my daily walks with the children, I ran the roads and hills and starved myself for the final month of my sojourn in France.

Joining the Gardaí

I felt the Gardaí was a natural place to start my career. I grew up surrounded by them, and the job was constantly praised by other family members, so I realized its security. Moreover, at a practical level, the pay was considered reasonable, and the contract was a long-term one—thirty years to be precise. I aspired to make a difference in society and combat crime while keeping my sights on opportunities of working in the Garda Press Office or Interpol.

I was happy to see my family on my return from France, although it wasn't long before I became somewhat irritated as my space became crowded again, and I found myself comparing my life in France to my life in Ireland. I felt guilty that I favored the French lifestyle and the comforts I'd been privy to and ashamed that I'd wished my parents had been able to afford to give us the same.

My parents were excited about my homecoming and the prospect of me joining the Gardaí; however, I had to pass the final stage of the process. I'll never forget doing the Irish oral interview. I was only a couple of days off the ferry from France. I wasn't prepared for the fact that having spoken mostly French for six months, I would have such difficulty speaking Gaelic when I needed it most. The interview was a shambles, and even though I managed to explain myself, I was convinced I'd failed. Next, I had to do a medical examination where my weight and height were checked. I was also nervous about the eye examination because I had always had to wear glasses for reading. Despite the sinking feeling in my tummy that continuing with the process was a waste of time, I still took the opportunity to walk up to the eye chart in the doctor's office and memorize it when the doctor conveniently left the room, just in case my *oh là là* had impressed earlier. This incident confirmed that I could achieve whatever I set my heart to, even when it wasn't straightforward and I might have to bend the rules a little bit.

Two weeks later, I got the news that I had been successful, and so began a new chapter in my life as a Garda recruit in the training college in Templemore.

The Assault

I was having an almost out-of-body experience sitting in a bar at 6 a.m. about to order a beer in celebration of completing a week of night duty. We didn't need much to celebrate in those days. The bar was a hive of activity with colleagues and marketers. It was an "early house," part of life for the market traders in Dublin. For a long moment, I began to question what I was doing and if I really wanted to drink alcohol. I realized I didn't actually like alcohol but couldn't understand why I continued to do something that I didn't enjoy. No sooner had I posed the question than I found myself caught up in the merriment and very soon assumed the role of the performing seal, one that often found me dancing on tables and singing into my beer bottle. However, an uncomfortable doubt about my lifestyle, career, and purpose had surfaced. It would revisit me many more times. I was feeling lost and empty, but I kept it to myself.

My career in the guards had potential. I had an opportunity to work at Interpol, and my grasp of French was valuable as the Gardaí were welcoming recruits with multiple language skills. They even sent me back to France to study French further with police personnel from all over the world. I was particularly impressed to be sitting beside a female officer from the CIA.

However, I left the guards after only an eight-year stint. I was disillusioned with society, how people were treated, and my lack of ability to make a difference given the restrictive nature of my role and lack of skills. One of my earliest memories of my disillusionment and disappointment was when as a young recruit, only a few weeks out of training, I was working in the leafy suburb of Donnybrook. We were basically security for the many embassies and ambassadors' residences in the affluent neighborhood. I detested it. It was a brain-numbing job and a colossal dampener of my enthusiastic spirit to change the world. The worst part was feeling so invisible and inconsequential as people walked past with barely an acknowledgment. It wasn't long before I began questioning my career choice. Where was the policing happening? That's all I wanted, not to be a security guard or remover of stray dogs from some of those manicured leafy gardens. I was soon transferred to the inner city, where more action and real police work were done.

Wanting the job since early childhood and accomplishing it easily made it more difficult to leave. It was a career in 1980s Ireland. There weren't many jobs, and no one was leaving the guards.

My inner voice was insistent that change was necessary. I also felt a constant yearning for more fulfillment and excitement. I still had yet to cross the pond, and the world was calling. All I could hear in my head was, "There has to be more to life."

It took an unfortunate incident, but one I can now say was necessary, to wake me up to more possibilities for my life and move on. I was working in plainclothes in a local task force when we pursued a stolen car one night. Joyriding was the trend at the time. After more than an hour of giving chase, the stolen car crashed head-on into a streetlamp.

The passengers of the car were about to escape when we gave chase. Just as I reached out to capture the backseat passenger of the stolen car, a uniformed colleague mistook me for one of the offenders, dragged me backwards, and beat me with a baton. I received at least three blows to the right side of my head.

I can still hear a voice shouting, "She's one of us! She's one of us!" The hitting stopped abruptly, and despite the sound of sirens and flashing blue lights from the multiple patrol cars that had now descended upon the scene, the night felt strangely quiet.

One colleague took me to the hospital, where I was later discharged and advised to see a neurologist. He revealed the name of the Garda who had assaulted me but warned me that nobody was willing to speak up about the matter, and they were not going to support me. I went home to the rented house I shared with some female colleagues feeling very confused and alone. What just happened?

Following advice from my doctor, I took a couple of weeks off work to recover. When I returned, I was met with unexpected hostility. Unkind verbal and written remarks about the incident pointed towards it being my fault. I was intimidated, to say the least, and shocked by the sudden change in how colleagues I considered friends were treating me.

It was clear that the colleague who had assaulted me was the one they wanted to protect. He was married with children, while I was single and childless. If he lost his job, his family would suffer. There was no regard for me. It was an easy contest for everyone to choose the winner.

Over the following weeks of enduring insults and dismissiveness, my self-confidence plummeted. The trust I had built with people dissolved, and I felt I couldn't trust anyone anymore. If I was going to get through this emotional onslaught, I knew I had to turn my attention inward and figure things out for myself. I had many unanswered questions, but I couldn't understand why colleagues I had considered to be friends turned their backs on me. I felt wronged and hurt.

The subsequent emotional trauma from how I was treated was much worse than any blow to my head and proved to be the catalyst for my departure from this career.

I have learned firsthand that when you ignore your soul's calling and guidance and stall on moving towards what you want, you might get a metaphorical blow to the head, or indeed a literal one, to make you pay attention and do something about it.

Telling my parents of my decision to leave a career, which at the time offered what most people saw as security in terms of longevity and income, was difficult. I was highly aware of how proud they were of me as I followed in my grandfather's footsteps. He had joined the force as one of the first recruits in 1922.

Panic and Peace

The night of the assault changed everything for me. Panic attacks in broad daylight while I was out walking the beat were becoming all too familiar. Running out of supermarkets while leaving my shopping in the trolley and hiding from people I knew became the norm. I told no one, and I thought there was something seriously wrong with me. Perhaps, in today's language, my distress might have been referred to as post-traumatic stress disorder.

The one person I could confide in was the neurologist. He was kind and attentive and eventually said the magic words to me on one of my visits. I broke down in his office and told him I felt so hurt and alone that I didn't know what to do. He looked me straight in the eye and said that I could do more with my life and that I should.

I stood up, and I thanked him. His words broke the spell that had for so long made me feel insignificant and not good enough as well as not allowing me to trust my intuition.

People, including relative strangers, can randomly become physical, breathing signposts on your life path, offering undoubtedly sage advice. I like to consider such people Earth angels, and I'm blessed to have encountered many in my life so far, including that neurologist. I felt that he saw me and cared about me. His words still echo in my head as he said compassionately on my final appointment, "What are you waiting for? You deserve so much more; you're capable of something better!"

I left his office liberated and on a mission to change the trajectory of my life. I knew it wouldn't be easy, but then in life, it is often the challenging things that are the ones we cherish most.

It was that sequence of events that gently pushed me forward in my life, and I have never regretted the decision I made that day. I always try to take the best from my life experiences and mostly remember the happier days, the many laughs, and how much the experience helped me grow as a person.

Serendipitously, I stumbled upon drop-in meditation classes in my neighborhood and could never have anticipated how crucial that moment would become. I had decided to leave the Gardaí. It was a secret as I was trying to work it all out. But I was in search mode, and those classes that had been previously invisible to me suddenly got picked up by my radar, and I found myself nervously inquiring about attending. Nothing was elaborate about these classes. The facilitator sat at the front of the room and invited us to close our eyes, focus on our breath, and leave whenever we wanted to. That was it, but it worked like magic. I now know that I was creating this much-needed space in my mind and allowing my imagination and intuition to guide me.

This was in the late 1980s, and meditation was not a common practice amongst my peers. But again, I was grateful to my dad; this brings me back to a memory of when he first introduced me to it a decade earlier in an attempt to calm my nerves before my school leaving certificate exams. We both went to a center in Dublin that taught yoga and meditation. Even though my dad knew nothing about meditation back then, he had read that it was helpful in overcoming stress, and he was looking for ways to help. But unfortunately, I felt very out of place in a room full of long-haired, bearded men sitting cross-legged, and so we left promptly. On reflection, a seed was planted, but back then, I was not remotely interested in being still or moving slowly, as running, netball, and a need for speed were ways for me to feel alive.

However, I believe in divine timing and that those meditation classes came to my attention when I needed them most. I loved how meditation made me feel, and I attended the classes whenever I could. The confusion I was feeling about the way I was being treated soon turned into clarity. I got clear about what I had to do, and I acquired the confidence to do it.

It was uncommon for a member of *An Garda Síochána* to leave the profession at this time, even if they had been wronged, but I knew my time there had come to an end. I was duly compensated, and that made leaving all the sweeter. On some level, I understood that this incident had happened *for* me rather than *to* me. It's a pity it had to end as it did. It's hard to know if I would have taken the plunge otherwise. This is something I may never know the answer to, but what I do know is that judging from the decisions that I have made in my life since I believe the likelihood is that I would have made that decision all over again.

Through this experience, I had the ability to prove to myself that I could do hard things and make those tough decisions when I needed to. I was exhilarated from choosing to free myself from a situation that no longer brought me joy. Looking back, I don't think I was brave, even though some colleagues admitted that they would have loved to leave but were too scared to. I was fueled by a sense of adventure, the bright lights of the big cities, and the pull to travel in style.

I found my power and inner strength and got back in the driving seat of my life. I hadn't a clue about the finer details of where this dramatic turn of events was taking me. All I knew was that nothing and no one was going to stop me. The inner voice was cheering me on, and that was enough for me.

CHAPTER 5

THE PATH OF PURPOSE

Don't ask yourself what the world needs.
Ask yourself what makes you come alive and
then go do that. Because what the world needs
is people who have come alive.

—Howard Thurman

Finding Purpose

The concept of having a purpose and living on purpose causes frustration in people's lives. Friends and clients often say, "I don't know what my purpose is. What does that even mean?"

Our lives have two primary purposes: to know that we are here to wake up to our spiritual nature and that we are here to use our unique gifts and talents to serve humanity.

Our purpose is a force from within that we bring to whatever we do: work, play, or change the world. It's a state of being that is present when we are asleep, awake, afraid, happy, reflective, practicing yoga, or when we are meditating. It's part of the fabric of who we are, our essence, and it becomes more magnified the more awake and aware we become. It has a presence that can make your heart skip a beat, like when you are in love. It's a feeling of intense excitement that might cause you to break out into song or dance or throw your hands up in the air while expressing an enthusiastic *yes*! At least, that's what I do from time to time, much to my son's embarrassment.

I've experienced this force when I'm walking in nature. I feel a deep connection with the trees, sky, ocean, sun, birds, plants, and fellow humans. It's the oneness, no separation. It's energy, and it's whispering to us all the time. Sometimes, when I'm walking my dog, I feel the wonder of the moment and tear up. Other times, the tears fall when I hear a song that pulls me back in time, reminding me of my eagerness as a teenager, impatient to grow up and be free. I quickly review my life in those moments and feel grateful for all the many adventures I've experienced.

Usually, I voice my deepest gratitude coupled with a bid for guidance on what I am to do next to help others. I often ponder these questions, "What do *you* want me to do? How can I best serve and make a difference?" I have learned that the secret is to be present, listen to the answers, and be guided by them. Once we are open to this awareness, we then have to be specific about what we are urged to do with our gifts and talents, recognizing how we can best use them to play our unique part in this world. When we get those moments of clarity and direction, the fire in the belly ignites, and it can feel electrifying.

My passion for helping others to feel that enthusiasm is absolutely part of my purpose. Nothing is more rewarding than seeing people begin to understand themselves at a deeper level, whether they be a friend or a client. With understanding comes power, and passion fuels this power to do our work and take responsibility for our lives while making a difference in a positive way. I have discovered that a perk of teaching others is that I get to learn twice.

As children, we live in our imagination and fantasize about being astronauts, ballerinas, nurses, doctors, and teachers. For many, that is where these fantasies remain, while others realize those dreams and love their life choices. We all know someone who seemed to *know* just exactly what they were born to do when in the womb as if they got a different memo from the rest of us on how to use their talents without the doubt and ignorance that keeps the majority of us stuck in reverse.

Perhaps my short spell as a ballerina explains this point nicely. In the early 1970s, I took ballet classes at the Morosini-Whelan Studio in Henry Street, Dublin. I was around seven or eight. It was a wonderful experience, and it felt so special to learn such a beautiful dance style. I was timid as a child and never fully expressed myself during the lessons or on a stage during a performance. I can still hear the critical voice in my head, holding me back just in case I made a mistake. I was terrified of making mistakes, and that fear stayed with me for many years. Thankfully, my views on mistakes, failures, and errors are very different today. But I developed a pattern of listening to that critical voice over the years, which held me back. I was terrified of looking foolish and being ridiculed, of being judged or rejected. It's interesting that my current mission is to help others face their fears and replace false beliefs with powerful truths to transform their lives. Through my work and personal growth, I've discovered that the feeling I had as a child of not being good enough is a universal issue for many. I'm so happy to have rewritten that script in my own life while helping hundreds of clients do the same.

My secret dream to emulate the beautiful English prima ballerina, Margot Fonteyn, could never happen. It is only in retrospect that we can see how we block ourselves and stand in our own way. As children, we don't filter out the negative very well because we have not yet learned the ability to see life outside of black and white. That comes later and through experience, so naturally, we accept whatever it is that our culture and environment teach us, and of course, we do not have the capacity to question. Suppose we were fortunate enough to be surrounded by forward-thinking people who praised and encouraged us to pay attention to the things that came naturally to us. We might feel more confident in pursuing our deepest desires.

I sometimes felt like a failure as I never excelled at anything I pursued. Being the lead dancer in *Swan Lake* was never going to be on my résumé. I didn't know that *grit*, as researched by the world's leading expert on the subject, Angela Duckworth, could be developed. Grit, she says, is the combination of resilience, ambition, and self-control in pursuing goals that can take months, years, or even decades to accomplish. It takes more than good genes to become a professional dancer or elite athlete. Commitment to doing whatever it takes physically and mentally is at the heart of their success. Having the mental toughness and perseverance to succeed is what sets the winners apart from the losers. In my work today, I often use the analogy of the Olympian to inspire my clients to adopt that attitude to make gains in their own lives. I'm proud to share that since the 2020 Olympics, I can refer to my young cousin, who won both a silver and gold medal in cycling. I've watched his success from afar but know the dedication, determination, and undeniable passion he possesses for his sport contributed to his Olympic stardom at age twenty-three.

Is This All There Is? Weighing My Options

As I got older and it became clear that I would not be earning a living as a professional dancer, musician, gymnast, athlete, or actress, the obvious and more attainable became my focus: to serve the nation as a guardian of the peace. This career choice was more familiar and something I believed I could do well. But as I explained previously, fate had other ideas, and my first encounter with anxiety was when I felt unfulfilled and dispirited as a Garda.

Aligned with the message I received as a child, "There is another way," I knew that change was beckoning and that I would find a new way to earn a living and find meaningful work. I wanted more than what I was experiencing in the Gardaí, and I knew I was meant for more. This doesn't mean that joining the force was a mistake, and many people find their personal fulfillment in this profession, but for me, it was an inevitable, necessary step. Even though there had been a number of red flags along the way, which I ignored, deep down, I knew I was not to have a long-lasting career with the guards.

Some of those signs came in the form of feeling restricted when helping criminals, whom I felt needed a different approach. Over the years, conversations with petty thieves, drug addicts, prostitutes, and the more hardened offenders always left me feeling bereft and incapable of making any positive impact on their lives. Not being able to offer them the help they needed because the job didn't allow for that was frustrating, to say the least.

Blessed to have had the upbringing I had, abundant with values and support, I could see that my life might have been very different if those standards had not been present. The job of a Garda is to maintain peace and order in society, apprehend offenders, and bring them to justice. However, I began to feel misaligned with those goals, not because I don't believe if you do wrong, there should be no punishment, but I had difficulty with the "them and us" dynamic and the inherent separation of one human from another. I was likely influenced as a child by having a prison and its residents as my neighbors. Many of the offenders I encountered felt remorse for their wrongdoing, and in the same breath, they felt trapped by their circumstances, often leaving us both feeling helpless.

Several of my colleagues suggested, often with a sneer, that I should have been a social worker and was in the wrong job. They were right. I knew I wasn't doing as good a job as I could because I wasn't enjoying the work in the way I had hoped. My favorite part of policing was as a community liaison officer, where I visited some of the elderly in their homes and enjoyed chatting about their lives. I loved being surrounded by the children in the inner city where I was based for a few years. Sometimes, I offered to help them with their homework, encouraging them to enjoy school. But mostly, I tried to instill an idea that they could have a better future if they believed in themselves more. I was a naïve twenty-one-year-old who felt trapped in a uniform.

A young boy always came to visit me when I was on security duty at the Special Criminal Court. He was handsome with blond curls and bright blue eyes. I found myself looking at him and thinking, "Wow! In a different place, at a different time, you could be one of those kids picked out of a crowd for your good looks and turned into a star." It would sadden me because I felt the hopelessness of the situation, which was compounded by my inability to do anything of much significance. The future was so predictable for him and his friends. Hundreds and thousands of children were just like him. When I asked him if his parents worked, he said they did. I asked him what they did, and his reply was, "They go to the pub." I felt great sorrow at that moment of realization that this innocent child thought that drinking in a pub was a job. I knew that the system was broken back then and that many people were being let down. I never thought that I could make a difference as I was also feeling something of a victim within the limitations of my chosen career, not a feeling I was proud of.

The frustration increased as the months turned into years, but the socializing always seemed to camouflage the dissatisfaction while keeping the idea of changing direction at bay. The desire for something different wouldn't go away. I wanted more life in my life, and I was determined to prove to myself and others that I could do more. The desire to break the mold and become a change-maker for myself and others was central to my decision. I never saw myself as a risk-taker, but I am.

Inherent in every decision to change is some form of risk, but when you weigh up the odds and look honestly at your choices, it can be far riskier to settle for something that appears safe yet makes you feel stuck. We look at how much it will cost us to make those changes without considering the cost of being stuck and settling for less than what we want. Fear of the unknown and unfamiliar grips us, but as author and psychologist Susan Jeffers says, we must "feel the fear and do it anyway." Growth resides in making necessary changes, taking risks, moving through challenges, and investing in personal development.

Flying High

Ever since the assault, my days within *An Garda Síochána* were numbered. I wanted out. I applied for a one-year leave of absence to keep my parents happy. I didn't fulfill the criteria for the request, but eventually, there was a hearing with senior officers. I outlined why I felt I needed and warranted the leave. They didn't disagree and gave me the leave, but not before they tried to convince me to stay by offering me something that would have been a dream come true a few years earlier—a position in the Press Office where I would have been liaising with the media regularly.

The offer of working in the Press Office was a good one and tempting to accept. However, it was too late. I was not going to be swayed. I knew it was time to move on. I wanted something more. I wanted to spread my wings. I wanted to see the world. I wanted to remove myself from the bubble that I had mostly lived in. I decided that working for an airline would be one job that could fulfill those ambitions.

London was calling, and so, twenty-four hours after I was granted my leave of absence, I was on my way to start a new career with British Airways as cabin crew.

While I was high on life, my decision was tough for my mother. I was full of the excitement of the unknown while she carried a deep-rooted memory of loss. She had seen her four brothers follow the same path to London and watched her mother heartbroken, awaiting their return. I felt my mother's pain, but I also wanted to be free and start over again.

Many colleagues thought I was mad to leave my secure, pensionable job to become a waitress in the sky. They'd ask, "Why do you want to spend your time just serving tea or coffee, chicken or beef? Where's the purpose in that?" All I could see was exotic and exciting places to visit and that I would get paid to be there. There was no contest between the two jobs. I felt some moments of guilt for abandoning my homeland and family, but my twenty-seven-year-old self wanted fun and adventure, and so, she won.

My career with British Airways delivered much more than I could have imagined because it opened my mind as I traveled the world. I met a vast array of fascinating people. I have served and spoken with movie stars, celebrities, royalty, and everyone in between. I have heard amazing stories and often sat with passengers during the night flights in the galley. Some were nervous, others restless, and many unhappy. The conversations were diverse, but invariably, I found myself giving unqualified advice to the overworked sales executive to renegotiate his contract or encouraging the love-struck Canadian journalist who was considering moving to Italy, where she had fallen madly in love, to just do it. It felt satisfying to offer help and to be regarded as a sounding board to these strangers. I didn't realize that I was being shown the possibility of another way to help people. I was guiding people on their journeys—and I don't mean just getting them to the correct departure gate as part of my role at the time but guiding people on their lives, and I loved it. It never struck me to take it further, but I was incredibly touched that anyone would value what I had to say. I guess this is how hairdressers and cab drivers feel—like accidental therapists, all in the name of doing a good job.

While I have seen hardship and poverty in the communities where I policed and the incredible wealth and affluence of some of my onboard guests, I witnessed the alikeness amongst us. We may seem to have little in common, other than that we are human beings trying to do our best with what we have. However, I believe we are much more alike than we are different. We each have a need to be seen and heard, to be accepted and be of use. No one wants to be judged or criticized, no matter who they are.

Nobody is perfect or has an ideal life. Even though I was somewhat awestruck with our guests, who were Hollywood A-listers, sports stars, and the like, I also read the newspapers and magazines back in those days and saw how they, too, received their share of abuse and negativity and had much to contend with.

This exposure to so many seemingly different people from all walks of life gave my life so much color. As I moved swiftly through airport after airport, from Heathrow to New Delhi or New York, I was reminded of my childhood dream of being a global citizen. I thrived on the constant thrill of traveling to different places surrounded by the incessant multilingual chatter of world travelers. I felt alive, connected, and hopeful. My former life seemed so closed in comparison to this vibrant and fast-paced one. I was grateful that I listened to my inner guidance and followed my heart.

The first time I crossed the Atlantic was one of the highlights of my life as the memory flooded back of when I stood with my dad at the water's edge in Connemara looking out at the horizon, with a vision of putting my feet on the ground in America. I couldn't help but think of the thousands who were forced to leave these shores at different times and for different reasons. Chicago did not disappoint. It was a *wow* experience, and I understood what everyone meant when they said everything in America was bigger: the cars, the streets, the skyscrapers, the attitude, the food, and the shopping. The American dream seemed available to everyone, even visitors. Visiting the States regularly made me believe that I could achieve my version of success. I'm grateful to the American authors and teachers who have helped educate me over the years and have implanted an attitude of self-reliance and possibility, fueling my commitment to personal growth.

~

CHAPTER 6

CLAIMING OUR DESTINY

The beauty of love is that in giving it away,
you are left with more than you had before.

—David Simon

Mister Right

One night, my fabulous friend and flatmate at the time persuaded me to accompany her to a lively nightspot we had often enjoyed. I didn't want to go, jaded as I was from a very late night of partying following an epic Eagles concert the night before. It was late and near closing time—almost 2 a.m., to be precise. I was doing what I always did on a night out after a few G&Ts, singing my old, reliable party piece "Summertime" into my make-believe mic, the empty bottle of tonic water. The usual revelers joined in, but then I noticed two guys standing there watching me sing. When I was finished, they applauded. One of them took the "mic" from my hand and sang back to me James Taylor's "You've Got a Friend." His name was Declan.

It was a different kind of wooing, I'll admit. He was looking at me intensely, and I had the strangest feeling that I had known him all my life. He was very charming, and he wasn't a bad singer either. He was a proud man from Portrush in Northern Ireland. I had never heard of Portrush, but he seemed unfazed. There was some chemistry . . . until he told me he was recently separated and had two young children. I was impressed by his openness and honesty, unlike many other men I'd met who were incapable of telling the truth about such matters.

Still, I thought, "Here we go again!" It seemed no single men were left on the planet. I strongly considered moving to Alaska, where I had heard there lived more men than women, who were looking for wives. Okay, I'm joking about Alaska, but you can imagine the frustration.

All I could think of was saying goodbye and continuing my search for Mister Right. While I'd had several relationships, I wasn't fortunate in love. I'd broken a couple of hearts in my time, but karma is always at work, and the boomerang rebounded on me too, leaving me a blubbering mess on a few occasions.

As I look back, I see a very naïve woman who wanted romance and a fairy-tale ending. I was tired of disappointing, meaningless relationships; yet, I remained optimistic. I was bored with alcohol, but I kept drinking. I was lonely in a crowd, but I kept partying. I was afraid of getting hurt again, but I kept hurting myself by foolish, mindless choices and excuses. The truth was that during those few years, the only "spirit" I was connected to was in a glass with ice and a slice of lemon.

So here I was, standing literally at a crossroads again— this time on Grafton Street—saying goodbye to Declan. We'd gotten on surprisingly well, given that my brain had switched off from any notion of letting this encounter go further. But something was different about him, and I found myself wondering if I should give it a go or regret it. He was very keen to see me again, and as he is a salesman at heart, you could say he sold himself to me that night.

The more we met, the more I liked him. He was a kind, thoughtful, compassionate person, and he loved me in a way that I had never experienced before. In many ways, he was the perfect partner . . . but it still bothered me that he was separated, not yet divorced, and had two young children.

When I joined British Airways in 1992, strange as it may seem, I had never met anyone who had been divorced. I had heard stories, and I had seen troubled relationships, but I didn't know anyone who had been divorced. Divorce was illegal in Ireland—a foreign concept in my world and not ever discussed honestly. The fear of being judged and ostracized always hung over people if they appeared to want something different or do something that rocked the status quo. In my new, open world, however, I was meeting people who had gone through troubled relationships, had remarried, seemed remarkably happy, and were neither ashamed nor guilty. I found this attitude to be liberating and refreshing. However, secretly, I never wanted to have that happen to me.

Once again, circumstances seemed to be testing my values and judgments. The situation was complicated, and it was not just about Declan and me. In the beginning, I found it difficult to allow myself to enjoy the relationship. I had to consider others and didn't want to bear guilt and shame for the rest of my life. I sometimes thought I should end the relationship before I became too embroiled in it. To my rational mind, it was not what I wanted, but I concluded it was what I needed for the evolution of my soul. The inner voice was whispering, "Give it a go; it's going to work out." Still, I wasn't jumping through hoops initially.

I had so many conflicting thoughts during this time. I was consumed with the fact I was being labeled an adulterer, albeit by a token few. It hurt, but then evidently, everyone concerned was hurting. The relationship felt doomed, selfish, and wrong. I hadn't erased the Catholic programming as entirely as I'd thought. The mental self-interrogation seemed endless. Did I break up a marriage? What if Declan hadn't met me? Should he go back and make it work? I didn't want to carry the burden of that responsibility, and the raw truth is that I didn't think I could handle the complexities of the relationship. It was aggravating that we weren't free to get on with our romance like everyone else. We had much to consider, and it often felt as if we were answerable to everyone else, explaining our lives away.

Torn, I told Declan several times that he needed to go back and restore his marriage. I didn't want to be a party to hurting innocent children. It wasn't their fault. I was at war with my morals and values, and the dilemma I found myself in haunted me. I was looking ahead, and the future didn't paint a pretty picture at times.

However, the more I urged Declan to leave, the more another part of me wanted him to stay. I knew there was always going to be more than just the two of us to consider in our relationship. Could I deal with that? I wasn't sure as I had heard so many unsavory tales from my new friends who were in a similar situation. People even suggested that at thirty-one years old, I was merely desperate to find a partner. Despite the challenges, Cupid was at work.

Telling my parents about the relationship wasn't easy. My father would never approve, and my mother's only concern was for my happiness. I felt as if I had to choose between my father and my boyfriend, which was difficult as I loved them both. My dad pleaded with me not to break the commandments and, out of concern for my salvation, reminded me that I couldn't tear a page out of the book of rules to satisfy my human needs. I felt shame and guilt. I was frustrated and angry. Mostly, I felt judged and that I was a disappointment. While many were wed and took the vow "till death do us part," not everyone kept that promise. People have their reasons for ending their marriages, and it's nobody's business except their own. I prayed a lot. I visited psychics and healers looking for answers. I lost trust in my inner guidance system. This was one of the most significant decisions of my life; I didn't want to have any regrets. I lived in my head mostly, but I eventually found my way back and chose to follow my heart. Even though I knew it wouldn't be easy, I trusted that we would find a way to make it work.

My intention at this time was to create a loving environment for the children when they would visit us. I loved them; they were beautiful and innocent. I was aware that they might hate me for being with their father, and I admit that I was scared I wouldn't be accepted. The idea of becoming a stepmother filled me with mixed emotions. The only stepmothers I knew of were the ones in the fairy tales, wicked and ruthless. While I knew I would never mistreat the children, I couldn't help but feel that I would be perceived as an intruder. Of course, that was my insecurity and immaturity surfacing. Nonetheless, the situation created an inner turmoil that I found hard to express in words.

We had arguments, mainly because I couldn't handle the situation at times. I was exhausted after a few months as I commuted between Dublin, London, the rest of the world, and Belfast. I was self-conscious and uncomfortable at times about the situation, and it eventually took its toll on me. My doctor prescribed antidepressants and counseling. I did both for about six months and decided I didn't want to be dependent on medication. I knew it wasn't going to resolve my problems. After some time off work, I reminded myself of what I had learned so many years ago. . . . There was another way for me to think about this situation, and I knew I had to have faith. We both believed we had come together for a good reason and knew we could work it out. *Just trust* was the constant whisper as if to say this was another opportunity to grow and prove that love always finds a way.

Tying the Knot in Vegas

We decided to get married in Las Vegas. It was 2003, and a boring registry office was not an option. No suitable alternatives were available in Ireland at the time. Anyway, Celine Dion and the Grand Canyon were far too enticing to miss. Little did I know that, once again, circumstances would conspire to challenge my choices.

As we boarded the plane in London, I felt very unwell. There were no clinking champagne glasses in our business class seats, a perk of the job. I could barely lift my head off the pillow and slept all the way to L.A. By the time I made it to Vegas, I could barely walk and was shivering, despite the sweltering heat. The next day, I was in a private medical clinic, having a 10-inch needle shoved into my spine. I needed to fight this unexplained virus.

Doubts about our imminent marriage began to surface. I found myself considering that this illness was a sign that I was making a big mistake. God would prevent me from getting married. I had made the wrong decision. You must remember I was delirious.

Thirty-six hours later, on my wedding day, I rose feeling better. I could stand; I could walk. The fever and the pain had gone. Now I could stride with confidence into my new life. The second-guessing was over.

We were staying at the Venetian Hotel, designed to resemble the city of Venice, replete with indoor canals and singing gondoliers. It was impressive with such visible signs of opulence and luxury everywhere. The wedding planner had done an excellent job, right down to getting me the perfect bouquet. I had spent the last few hours getting my hair and makeup done before we left the room hand in hand, nervously making our way through the crowd to the wedding gondola. As we walked through the lobby, listening to the good-hearted well wishes from staff and guests, even though I smiled in acknowledgment, I couldn't help but feel a familiar loneliness consume me.

While I had never dreamed of the big white wedding, I did like the idea of my dad giving me away. Over the years, Declan and his children had become part of our family, but my father's devoutness was unwavering. I felt a pang of guilt as if I had betrayed my dad and denied him the pleasure of that experience. Still, I also knew that I had to take full responsibility for my life and my choices. This was my life. I must make my *own* rules. I convinced myself that my dad would love me no matter what and that he would accept my decision one day. And so, I was able to return to the moment devoid of doubt. This was my moment. This was our moment. Love will always win.

We stepped onto the gondola along with our wedding planner and eucharistic minister, who was there to bless us. We floated blissfully on the water, serenaded by our singing gondolier and celebrated by the delighted onlookers and street performers. It was magical.

After a beautiful dinner, we danced the night away. I met some gorgeous Venezuelan women who became my makeshift bridesmaids, vying for the bouquet I threw over my head. We had the most exquisite evening.

Getting married and honeymooning in the entertainment capital of the world was thrilling. From front row seats at Cirque du Soleil and Lord of the Dance to being voted the best-dressed couple on the night we attended an intimate concert with Celine Dion, we felt very celebrated and grateful. Another highlight and a bucket list wish fulfilled was the epic plane ride over the Grand Canyon. Eating our lunch of rice and beans prepared by members of the Havasupai Indian tribe felt very special, as we sat mesmerized by this sacred wonder of the world. With my fear of heights at the time, I had to lie on my belly to glimpse the famous mile-deep gorge below. It was dizzying but spectacular, an experience to cherish forever.

Two weeks later, we were back in Ireland. It was my birthday, and our wedding celebrations continued as we partied and mingled with family and friends. My father chose not to come, and we respected his decision. Even though according to some, we were not free to love one another and had broken a biblical rule, we believed that love would save the day. We just had to keep the faith and trust that we'd work things out no matter the circumstances. Determined and in love, we began a new chapter. We faced our problems with an attitude of surrender and a strong belief that we were meant to be together.

CHAPTER 7

GOD'S PLAN

What you think, you become. What you feel,
you attract. What you imagine, you create.

—Anonymous

My Son

We had been married a little over two years when, at forty-one years young, I found myself living in a moment of pure joy with my baby son, Finn, in my arms.

As I mentioned earlier, more than twenty years prior to this, a doctor told me that I would find it difficult to have children, and it was doubtful that I even would. Several other doctors emphasized this forecast over the intervening years. I did not know much about the power of the mind back then, but I'm so glad that while I *heard* the doctor's words that could have influenced my fate, I *listened* instead to my inner voice, the part of me that knew I could get what I wanted.

You might be wondering what warranted a visit to the doctor and why he was so convinced that motherhood might not be an option. It was simply a case of my menstrual cycle being erratic, and with no medical tests carried out, the conclusion was purely based on assumptions of a negative nature.

It might have taken twenty-three years to disprove their prognosis and prove my self-hypnosis, but I was one elated mama either way. I hasten to add that I am very grateful to medical professionals for their help in making my dream a reality, but I also take some credit for steering them to use their gifts with my persistence and determination. Following several painful miscarriages, including my son's twin, fertility treatment was the answer, along with a positive and healthy mindset. I was glad I had nurtured this way of thinking as it has come in handy on many occasions, including when the friendly nurse who was given the job of artificially inseminating me casually suggested, "I have to say to you that this probably won't work; don't get your hopes up." She chose to say this upon the insertion of the magic potion, my husband's seminal fluid, whilst I lay there, legs akimbo.

Really? As if this wasn't confronting enough?

I brushed her thoughtless remark away with the deft movement of my left hand, and once more, the inner voice of my soul spoke to me, "Relax, don't let it in. You know it's going to happen; you are going to hold your baby soon." Then a not-so-gentle voice inside my head commented, "You're paying to get pregnant with these people? They are taking your money and telling you this?" I knew better than to entertain this voice, the inner critic at work, often disguised as my loyal supporter but with an undertone of doom and gloom if given too much scope. And so, I listened to the true inner voice that whispered, "Breathe . . . visualize . . . have faith . . . just relax . . . stay positive . . . you're so close... this will work out!"

While I've always been very aware of this constant, invisible aspect of myself encouraging and guiding me, I rarely spoke about it. I have since discovered that I have been an unconscious competent for most of my life, working with the laws of the universe without realizing it.

Trust, Belief, Faith

Enter *trust, belief, faith*—the key components in living your life with the conviction that all is happening for your highest good. The setbacks and obstacles are part of the process. How each of us handles those setbacks depends on our level of awareness and determines our levels of joy and happiness. I believe we have the power to create a beautiful life and that when things don't seem to be going our way, it's because something even better is on the horizon. This approach to life has helped me enormously, not least when I suffered my first miscarriage.

I was working on the flight to Johannesburg and looking forward to a day of pampering at the beauty salon in the classy Sandton City mall. After several wonderful treatments, I stood up and felt quite dizzy. After a trip to the bathroom, it looked like my long-awaited period had arrived, and my appointment with the gynecologist for the following week seemed less urgent. By the time I hailed a cab to take me to the hotel, I was doubled over in pain. This was a car ride from hell, not only due to the evening rush hour traffic but also because I was now hugging the passenger seat from behind while trying to stifle a very unfamiliar sound so as not to completely frighten the wide-eyed young driver, who looked at me as if he had had the misfortune of carrying a woman possessed. One hour later, I tumbled out of the cab and climbed the hotel steps on all fours, screaming for a doctor.

Soon after, my worst fears were confirmed when the doctor revealed that I was having a miscarriage. It was horrific. The bathroom looked like a murder scene, and my hysterical, incomprehensible calls to Declan and my mother were among the most difficult I'd ever made. I couldn't make sense of what had just happened. I was in complete shock. I didn't know that I was pregnant.

They sent an ambulance, and while I was putting things together for the hospital, I almost passed out as I paused to consider *what* I had carelessly flushed down the toilet. Questions flooded my mind: How long was I pregnant? And was it a boy or a girl? How was I ever going to find out now?

It was suggested later that I may have been sixteen weeks pregnant, but the gender was unknown. During the three days of my stay in the hospital, I could think more clearly, and despite my loss, I felt relief. I could get pregnant. The doctors were wrong. I was right; I knew it. If it happened once, it could happen again, and I held on to this idea wholeheartedly. God had a plan for me. I like to think he has a calendar of events, and when the time is right, provided you and I play our part in the co-creation of our dreams, all will unfold in divine timing.

My faith was strengthened, and I could more consciously prepare my mind, body, and soul for motherhood. I began connecting to the soul of my baby when I meditated, prayed, and went for my walks. I visualized myself as pregnant. I felt pregnant. I rubbed my imaginary bump. I saw myself holding my baby. I could smell that new baby smell and feel the softness of his skin as I kissed his cheek. I experienced two further miscarriages, but I kept believing. I was getting closer and closer to a deep, burning desire materializing, and I continued to imagine what it felt like to be a mother.

As Napoleon Hill states, "Whatever the mind of man can conceive and believe, it can achieve."

It can be said in many ways, but this one idea can be the key to our success or failure: we become what we think about. Our thoughts either support or sabotage us at any moment and determine whether we attract or repel what we want. I knew with all my heart that I would succeed in my burning desire to become a mother. I simply wouldn't entertain any other idea.

Belief in what is not yet visible is crucial. Many people need to see it to believe it, but the reverse is true. First, you must believe it, and then you will see it. That's what Napoleon Hill is indicating to us. If you use your imagination in conjunction with unwavering belief, what you want will manifest when you see yourself being, doing, or having it. There is, however, a caveat; you must fall in love with the idea.

Becoming emotionally involved with your heart's desire and having an unshakable expectation of it being realized is part of the secret. I would go further and suggest you need to be obsessed with managing your emotional state, feeling what it's like to achieve your dream and keeping your vibe high while holding the vision of your intended outcome in your mind. Little else occupied my mind. I didn't realize that I was finding my own evidence of how to manifest my deepest desires, something I now teach my clients to do. Theory is one thing, but taking something from conception to accomplishment is, in reality, an entirely different teaching. I did not know back then that the mind thinks in pictures, and I was creating a gallery of them.

To illustrate this idea, answer this question: think about your front door. On which side of the door is the lock? Most likely, you got a flash of your front door and found yourself going through the motions of putting your key into the lock, as you have done automatically hundreds of times, in order to answer this question correctly. Am I right? So, you can see that your mind thinks in pictures. If I say the words "Mona Lisa," you will get another flash of the painting by Leonardo da Vinci. You might even imagine yourself standing in front of the painting itself, if you've been to the Louvre Museum, and then you imagine the Eiffel Tower, seeing picture after picture in your mind. Even thinking about what you want to eat for dinner floods your mind with images. When you're being deliberate in creating images or movies in your mind of what you want, you're programming your subconscious mind to see into the future—what life can be like with your wish fulfilled.

Whatever your goal is, the first step is to believe you can have it and then picture it as clearly as possible in your mind using your five senses. Notice the sounds you can hear as you think about the result you want to reach. While you continue to replay this movie often, you're training a part of your brain to act like a goal-seeking device, moving you towards what you focus on and it towards you. Now we know why whatever we focus on is magnified and manifested, good or bad. Your brain is seeking out what you are paying attention to. This is why you need to be ultra-aware of what you're feeding it in terms of your focus. I think it takes the woo-woo out of how the law of attraction works. Remember, it's just as easy to get what you want as it is to get what you don't want. It's all about where your focus lies. What are you focusing on? Are you focused on the presence of your wish fulfilled or the lack and scarcity of it?

In my case, I was laser-focused, so much so that I saw pregnant women everywhere I went, and this helped me to increasingly visualize myself in the desired state. Even though I felt pangs of envy at times, I knew feeling that way was not going to help me, so I'd quickly change my mindset and focus on the cherub who was on the way.

Whether it's a baby, business, or relationship you want, the same rules apply, and the best part is in understanding that we do not need to know in what way it's going to happen or when; just trust that it will. Some of you may be thinking that what I'm saying is exaggerated and that maybe I must be *lucky* because you may not have found the same results. However, I know for sure that we are all capable of manifesting what we want when we learn the principles of creation and apply them to our lives. We must always add the caveat that we're open to receiving something even better so that if things don't appear to go our way, we must trust that there is a reason. It's not enough to read the books and attend the seminars. Knowledge is only potential power, but without implementation, it's ineffective, and sadly, this is where many of us fall short. I have discovered from working with hundreds of clients that despite wanting changes in their lives, they don't believe that they can achieve them, let alone deserve them.

People know far more than they demonstrate, but they create a gap between what they want and what they have by not doing what they know how to do. It's been said that the average person uses less than 10 percent of their potential. Fear, limiting beliefs, and bad habits stand in the way of making giant leaps in their lives. We get stuck, frustrated, and trapped in a mental prison of our own making. That's where our work begins. Understanding the repetitive patterns that hold us back and creating a paradigm shift to freedom becomes the goal.

As little children, we form beliefs about ourselves according to our upbringing and the environment in which we grew up.

Oftentimes, our beliefs are the beliefs of our parents, carers, schoolteachers, or neighbors; however, we then make these beliefs our own. Furthermore, we interpret some negative situations subjectively, often blaming ourselves for things that were way outside our control but left us feeling vulnerable. Those beliefs make us who we are. In other words, we see ourselves as either confident, worthy, and capable of following our dreams and making changes in our lives without the need for approval, or we hold an image of ourselves as someone who is not good enough, lacking self-esteem and confidence. The latter causes us to hide our true essence from the world. We hold ourselves back. We feel invisible and often worthless. We convince ourselves that our dreams are just that, dreams, futile. We fear rejection, judgment, and criticism from others, yet that is exactly what we do to ourselves. When we grow up, we're either the one who is living the dream or the one watching someone else live it.

The good news is that if we don't like the results we're getting in our lives, we can change them. It begins with identifying the patterns of thinking that have been ingrained in the subconscious mind. Your subconscious mind is running the show. Every memory of every event in your life is recorded there. Every thought you believe, whether right or wrong, resides there. Your thoughts are causing you to feel a particular way, which affects your choices and, ultimately, your results. Changing your behavior alone is *not* the answer. You must change the thinking and beliefs behind the behavior to successfully achieve different results. Equally, changing your thoughts without changing your behavior is not enough. We need to believe and act as if what we want already exists, because it does.

As I've already mentioned, everything is energy; energy is all there is in one form or another. Sometimes, energy is referred to as a frequency or vibration. Our thoughts are energy, and when we're in the co-creative process, we must become a vibrational match to the very thing we want.

The quickest way that I know to get into alignment vibrationally is through the practice of gratitude. Being grateful for what we have already helps us to raise our moods and open our hearts. *Feeling* grateful is more powerful than just *thinking* of things to be grateful for. It should be a visceral experience that brings tears of appreciation and love to our eyes. We become a magnet for more of the same because what we appreciate appreciates in value, quantity, and worth. Gratitude, prayer, meditation, trust, expectation, and some fertility intervention were my combined ingredients for success in becoming a mother. And there were plenty of tears.

God's plan did not end there for me, as you will see.

⁓

CHAPTER 8

JUST PAUSE

Self-reflection is the school of wisdom.

—Baltasar Gracián

State of Flow

Many years ago, I was on holiday with my husband in Australia at the Great Barrier Reef. It was a dream come true to experience another wonder of the world and realize a wish on my bucket list. Encouraged by the excitement of the other adventurers onboard the vessel that anchored us close to the reef, I jumped into the open water.

The first thing that I noticed was the stillness of the water. Except for the giddy enthusiasm of the other divers and snorkelers, it was strangely calm and silent. I was treading water in an upright position in an ocean so vast with so many secrets and treasures buried right below me.

As I put my face in the water and positioned the floating noodle around my body so that my flippered feet could keep me afloat, I gasped at the spectacle before me. After what seemed like an eternity of watching the technicolored display of life below the surface of this great ocean, a new awareness began to emerge, possibly prompted by the realization that the reef was now grazing my knees. I felt like I was in a meditative flow state, transfixed in an ethereal world. As I raised my head and looked around, I saw that I had drifted more than a hundred feet from the boat, and the worst part was that I couldn't see one other person.

You can imagine the movie playing in my mind at that precise moment and my simultaneous regrets for having watched too many movies with such scenes in which I now found myself. The only sound I could hear was my heart beating like a drum, or should I say, a tuba, as I tried to compose myself and move towards the boat. The theme song from *Jaws* (duuuunnnn duun . . . you know the rest) was pumping in my veins. I thought at that moment that I was going to die.

As quick as I could, I made my way towards the boat, having taken just one big gasp of air. As I moved closer, all I was aware of was the pain in my chest and a repetitive mantra of "Dear God, help me; I don't want to die! Help me! Please don't let the sharks eat me . . . please. Oh God, I'm sorry for everything I've done that displeased you, and I promise to be a better person. *Please, God!*"

It was not my expiry date on that day, and as I clambered the dangling ladder, wobbly and hypoxic, my mantra and prayer turned to "Thank You, God, thank You, thank You, *thank You!*" The relief was immense, and all I wanted was to find my husband, exchange stories, and tell him how much I loved him. I was thankful to hear the sound of life, which was so welcome, as other people were finishing their dives and climbing excitedly on board too.

I share this story as an analogy. I mentioned before about drifting aimlessly in life and how we may encounter some unwelcome surprises. After being in the open water of the Pacific Ocean that day, I reflected on what had happened. I was careless about my safety. I blindly jumped out of the boat without thinking about any potential danger or where I was going. Captivated by the breathtaking beauty below the water, I didn't lift my head to see where I was in relation to the boat. So, in a short time, the current pulled me along, and I didn't know, or much less think, I was drifting way off course.

I was blessed that day to get away with two grazed knees, discomfort in my chest, and some sunburn on my shoulders. It is a great lesson and metaphor for explaining how important it is to be prepared for when something unexpected pops up to "bite" you. And it will.

Life is full of tests, and at any given moment, we are either passing or failing those tests depending on our level of awareness, our commitment to personal growth, and whether we are facing the challenges or avoiding them.

Self-Reflection

I took time to reflect on my experience at the reef. Do you ever take time to hit the pause button to reflect on your life, happiness, and inner peace? Are there some areas where you feel as if you've hit the jackpot, while in other areas, it feels as if you've hit rock bottom? Panic not! It's simply time to check in on yourself. Self-reflection is an empowering activity, opening us up to greater insights and wisdom available only during these more contemplative moments.

Evaluating Your Life

Consider treating self-reflection as if you are taking a life audit, or you might prefer life appraisal. Without meaning to be gloomy, you might want to ask yourself this one question Steve Jobs asked himself daily: "If today were the last day of my life, would I want to do what I am about to do today?" If he answered no too many times, he knew he needed to change something.

When you ask yourself that question, what's your answer?

Life is too short to do something continuously that drains your resources, that's uninspiring and unfulfilling. While I didn't ask myself that exact question when I knew my days were numbered in the guards or the other areas of work I was engaged in, I felt strongly that I must not stay where I no longer felt inspired or free to express my natural talents, which are the gifts of my soul. I can go so far as to say that I was being asked the questions from within. I'd often hear, "You are not fulfilled here, so why do you stay?" or "This isn't what you really want. Don't you think it's time to make some changes?"

The truth is, I was institutionalized back then. But don't we all become that way? Whether it was work or everyday life, knowing what I needed to do at what time and on what day, my life was controlled by my duty roster. While there is so much value in such organization of one's time, it can be quite stifling, restrictive, and robotic.

If you want something you've never had before, you're going to have to think in new ways. The benefit of deliberately checking in on yourself and becoming your own private investigator is that you are in the driving seat of your life. You get to direct your life rather than have it direct you. By consciously evaluating your life, you will raise your awareness and be able to distinguish between what your soul wants you to experience versus what your ego wants. The ego is the part of you that encourages you to remain in the status quo. It lives in fear of change and will remind you of all the reasons why you shouldn't even try to alter the course of your life. It's consumed with our identity in terms of our status in life and wants us to compare ourselves to other people. This is destructive and potentially detrimental to our wellness and happiness and the ultimate betrayal to our soul's agenda.

As you awaken to the direction towards which your soul is guiding you, you recognize that so long as you're concerned with what everyone else is doing, you are not creating your own life. You become familiar with the guidance from your gentler voice, your soul. It's time to explore your "calling," what your soul is here to express through you.

Consciously evaluate your time so you can, as Caroline Myss says, "put your spirit to use in the world." However, this takes time, belief, vision, and persistence. It's a journey of constant introspection and adjustment.

The more a person drifts along nonchalantly, ignorant of their power to create their own circumstances and economy, the greater the chances of encountering unwelcome surprises. Be prepared. Manage your mind continuously, challenge your thoughts, connect with the wisdom of your heart, and align with your soul's truth. You can steer the ship that is your life and aim it in the direction of your soul's deepest desires.

Reflecting on What's Working and What's Not

Life itself can feel like a Groundhog Day of tedious, repetitive habits and routines. Even when we're bored and feel robotic, it's often easier to continue doing the same old, same old, sometimes expecting a different result, and you know how that old saying ends. It doesn't have to be this way. You deserve the life you feel called to live.

Whether you find yourself anxious or depressed at how you ended up where you are or have a hunch that there's something better for you, the power of self-reflection can help you to create space before making your next move. Take this time to look at the things that are working in your life and those that are not. Refine things. Make necessary changes based on what expands you. You are meant to live an extraordinary life. Start believing it and act.

Reflecting on the Important Questions

If you want to see improvements in your life, you must master yourself first. It's time to ask yourself some powerful questions. I mentioned earlier that the answers are always in the questions. Think about how much easier it is to get the answer and information you want when you ask Google a straightforward, concise question. When trying to figure out issues and make better life choices, starting to look for solutions is more effective than mulling over problems and painful past circumstances.

Of course, expert help is sometimes necessary. A counselor, coach, or therapist needs to ask questions to help unravel the cause of their client's or patient's problems. The police must ask a thousand questions during a criminal investigation. It's the same during any kind of job interview or when you are being coached. Don't be afraid of the answers. I've had several clients tell me that they're anxious about the answers because they may have to make significant changes. I always tell them that their freedom is just on the other side of their fear of change, and it's true. And when I observe them experiencing that truth firsthand and making strides in their lives, I know I am not making this up.

Below are the four questions that changed my life.

I was introduced to this conversation with my soul when I was at the Seduction of Spirit retreat with Deepak Chopra, and I've never stopped having it. You can ask these questions at the beginning of your meditation practice or anytime throughout the day. Make yourself comfortable. Sit up tall, relax your shoulders, close your eyes, and take three deep breaths in through your nose and out through your mouth. (Make the sound "haaaa" as if you're fogging a mirror as you exhale.) Bring your awareness to your heart's center, the seat of your soul, and ask the following questions:

1. Who am I? Listen. . . .
2. What do I want? This can be of a material, physical, mental, or spiritual nature. Again, listen. . . .
3. What is my dharma (purpose)? (And, as part of that same question, How can I help? How can I serve?) Listen. . . .
4. What am I grateful for? Allow the answers to surface spontaneously.

Don't force the answers, and don't be concerned if you don't get them immediately. Some may come to you when you least expect them and in very creative ways. God has a sense of humor; be open to the miracles awaiting you as you continue to engage in this dialogue with your divine essence and uncover your truth. If you practice this daily, you will experience a remarkable shift in your awareness, and answers to long-term problems will emerge. An inner peace rises from within, replacing an emptiness that can never be filled with quick fixes and external things.

This practice has helped me to be comfortable with wanting something better in life. I learned that the purpose of my soul is to serve and give. While I've often felt selfish and foolish for wanting to do more trainings and programs to improve my skills, it has helped me to understand that our spirit is always open for expansion and fuller expression. This means that our desires, dreams, and wishes are the forces that incite our growth from which we create more joy, abundance, and fulfillment.

This self-inquiry practice has been key in helping me to uncover the path to my purpose. It led me to train in multiple methodologies, where I grew in confidence and gained increasingly more clarity as to how I could best serve humanity. This is ongoing, and it excites me. I feel alive and driven to honor my soul's purpose every day and create my own soul-guided business. It's a staple for my spiritual fitness, and I know how disconnected I feel when I let it slip. Give it a go for yourself and pay attention to what happens.

On a practical level, posing these questions allows you to begin noticing your life more and develop more awareness of where you need to prioritize your time and what changes you need to make. Checking in on yourself helps to keep you on track with your purpose and goals. Just as the rocket needs to course-correct for the majority of its time on the way to the moon, you and I can do the same with our lives. If something isn't working, we can adjust or fix it. If we can't fix it, we can change it. We can take responsibility for keeping ourselves in a beautiful flow state. Focusing primarily on what you wish to accomplish without complaining about its absence keeps you in flow. If you want something different, you have to *do* something different and *be* something different, even if it might be uncomfortable. Find the path that lights you up and continue moving towards that light.

Reflecting on the Use of Your Time

Please note, none of the following questions are meant to cause shame but to help you think about how you're using your time: Do you spend your time wisely? Do you procrastinate, constantly thinking that it's not the right time to act? Are you waiting for someone else to validate you? Do you get distracted easily? How much time do you spend online following other people's lives? Do you believe you have all the time in the world or that you never have enough? Are you organized, focused, and disciplined? Do you know where you're going in life? Who is holding you accountable? Are you deceiving yourself with low expectations, neglecting your goals and dreams? Are you settling for more of the same and less than you deserve?

I've learned that we can't manage time, but we can manage our activities, which allows us to make adjustments to improve our situation. We each have the same 1,440 minutes every day. While we cannot add more time to our days, we can manage our use of it. Being more organized means being less stressed. Being less stressed means being more productive. Being more productive allows space for being more creative. Being more creative increases our likelihood of more joy, fulfillment, and inner peace.

I appreciate time and its value, and nowadays, I am much more discerning about what I take on. However, I have wasted so much time at different stages of my life where I have massively procrastinated. I have been lazy and have settled often, and then I'd get a jolt of motivation and find that I'd enthusiastically overcommitted to things, taking on too many tasks, thinking I could get them all done, only to feel exhausted and disappointed in myself. Wasting time affected my confidence as the inner critic boldly informed me that I was a failure and could do nothing right. Does that sound familiar? Still, regretting how you wasted time in the past is pointless. Today is a fresh start. We can't turn back the clock, but we can make better decisions going forward. Time is precious and waits for no one. It warrants our undivided attention so we can make every moment count. *Someday* is not a day of the week. None of us knows how much time we have left. It's a sobering thought. Let us make a move!

Self-Empowerment

Empowerment through Taking Responsibility

As you reflect on what's important, you'll realize your whole life has brought you to this point. Nothing is wasted, and there are no failures; it's all learning or simply feedback. This empowers you to know that you don't have to stay stuck in unsupportive and toxic relationships. You act on the messages from your body, get yourself checked out, and move on to pastures new from roles that deplete you. You get to decide how you spend your time and with whom. You accept that the only opinion that matters when it comes to choices in your life is yours. Your capacity for growth increases, and you know that you can never quit your calling. You're never too old to honor it, and you're most definitely good enough to actualize it.

Instead of complaining about some of the unpleasant results that you are getting in your life, decide to do something about them. Commit to shifting your energy to a higher vibration and activate your deepest desires by becoming the person you need to be in order to achieve them.

The blame game is a further waste of time and energy. Yet too many of us whine about the unfairness of life and how our problems are always someone else's fault. They live in victimhood. This is a potentially dangerous place; if that's where you live, I'd encourage you to move out fast.

On that day in the water on the Great Barrier Reef, I had no one to blame except myself. When we take responsibility for our lives, we are back on board, retaking the helm, choosing which way to go and course-correcting where necessary.

Another way we disempower ourselves is by letting others' opinions of us influence what we do or don't do with our lives. We need to value our own opinion, politely ignore the naysayers and critics, and once and for all, do what we want boldly and without apology. Set healthy boundaries. There's no need to argue or fall out with anyone just because they don't agree with your choices. Don't spend too much time wondering about how much they're thinking about you. We overthink this, and the harsh truth is that most people are so caught up in their own troubles and lives that they aren't thinking about you for very long. Take responsibility for making your own choices and let no one steal your dreams.

Empowerment through Meditating

Walking in nature, reading, practicing yoga, and meditating are my go-to rituals to recalibrate and decompress from stressful situations. These activities act as maintenance tools. I see each of them as a spiritual practice, sacred. I like to say, "Go outside to connect inside." It works every time.

Meditation is healing. It releases accumulated stress and slows down the aging process. Below are other benefits I have found through daily meditations that emphasize how vital it can be in helping us to awaken to our greatness.

- Our awareness expands, and the spell under which our false self rules becomes broken.
- We begin to recognize that we are more than the person we see in the mirror.
- A shift occurs as we stop settling for a life that no longer brings us joy and opt for one that elates and inspires us.
- We become more observant of our thoughts and begin to view the events in our life as an objective witness, allowing us to be more perceptive.
- We trust that a solution is always available.

- We begin to see the oneness in all things when we go beyond the limited version of ourselves dominated by our ego and mind.

- We tap into our heart and connect to the energies of peace, harmony, laughter, and love and keep them circulating in our life.

- Our inner space expands, allowing for more nourishing choices, ensuring the best outcome for all concerned.

- We become more accepting of others and where they are on their journey and their level of awareness.

- We begin to see the innocence in our fellow humans, which allows us to be more patient and forgiving.

- We connect to the whispers of our soul, deepening our sense of belonging and higher purpose.

- We trust that there is a reason when things don't appear to go our way.

- We become more conscious of how our actions affect our life and appreciate our expanded awareness to manifest easily.

- Our inspiration increases within the silent spaces between our thoughts, bringing a real sense of happiness to the surface.

- We begin to cultivate a deeper appreciation of our existence and our life purpose.

Empowerment through Mindset Change:
From Limitation to Abundance

So many of us live in automatic pilot mode when it comes to our life, with a default program set to lack and limitation. We may want change but resist it at the same time. Our resistance causes us to feel stuck, helpless, and afraid. We continue to allow past disappointments to shape our future as we don't place enough faith in achieving what we want, choosing instead to expect not to succeed. We often think we do not have any other option; however, we do. When you take the time to get to know yourself and understand that you live in an abundant universe, you begin to see things differently. Dr. Wayne Dyer said that "when you change the way you look at things, the things you look at change." This outlook epitomizes an abundance mindset. You remain open to the flow of creative solutions, guidance, and opportunities coming your way.

The mind is always paying attention to the words you say to yourself. Those words create pictures, as I've mentioned before. When I described my experience earlier, you saw pictures in your head of a woman in the open water, and you also saw sharks and other potentially dangerous sea creatures. Am I right?

Now, reflect on your circumstances. What movie are you running in your head about your life? Are you in real danger, or is it imagined? Even in my case, I was not in any imminent danger, but I perceived I was. This thought shifted my body into a stress response.

As I replayed my *personally directed* movie in my head, I realized how much I had added to my stress. It was *not* the time to be visualizing sharks circling my hyperventilating body or to see the possible consequences of that. When you're the director of your mind, you can put anything into that life movie and make it real.

Now, be careful as those movies can be scarier than real life for most of us. We tend to fill our minds with what might happen, thinking of the worst-case scenarios instead of asking ourselves if what we're thinking is accurate, true, and supportive. If only we created movies in our minds about what we do want with such attention to detail and intensity, we'd soon be manifesting geniuses. Sadly, all too many of us are convinced that we're not good enough or deserving to have what we want. We incorrectly believe we've reached our upper limits. This becomes the story in the movie we watch over and over again in our mind, which, unless edited, becomes a self-fulfilling prophecy.

Why do we do that to ourselves? It goes back to our conditioning in childhood and the assumptions we came to about our place in the world based on the experiences that we had and the people around us. Without ever challenging our stories or knowing our truth and potential, we live in ignorance of our greatness. Ignorance leads to fear, and fear is the real culprit that triggers what's known as the fight or flight response in our brain. We can thank our ancestors when they chose either to flee from a physical threat or fight it. This response is still activated by our brains today but mostly from mental threats caused by our thinking. We can have a full-blown panic attack in our own bed following a viewing of our mind-made movie where we are acting out an imaginary scenario that appears real.

Empowerment through Destressing

During my adventure on the Great Barrier Reef, my breathing shortened, my heart pumped faster, the stress hormones were releasing adrenaline and cortisol into my bloodstream, and the systems in my body responsible for digestion and antiaging, amongst others, shut off. (I mean, who needs antiaging hormones when you're about to expire? How clever is our body?) This physiological reaction occurs when we perceive ourselves to be under attack, and our ancestors reacted the same way. We're no longer fleeing wild animals or other tribes as we did in our caveman days. Yet, we can get into this state fast by just thinking about having to present at a work meeting or reacting to our flight being delayed, for example. All reason goes out the window, and we're left feeling vulnerable and incapacitated.

Our body is intelligent and designed to support us in living an extraordinary life, but we are often ignorant of its capability and abuse and despise it simultaneously.

Too many of us live in a constant state of stress, afraid and disconnected from our authentic Self. It is vital to discern between the real and the unreal, to challenge our limitations and celebrate our uniqueness. Projecting our life into some future event and worrying that we won't cope or will make mistakes causes anxiety. We send ourselves into a tailspin. We are not working with our intuition. We are ignorant of our power to choose something that will resolve our situation favorably. We are unaware of the laws of the universe and how our intuition communicates with the Infinite Intelligence that knows all things. The subconscious mind, often referred to as the universal mind, cannot distinguish between real and imagined. If you grasp this idea, you can use it to your advantage.

To deal with stress, we need to stop directing imaginary movies of a negative nature. You are the one who oversees your life and can accept or reject your thoughts and beliefs. To overcome this anxious feeling and come back to what is *real*, such as the breath in your body, focus on consciously breathing and ground yourself in the awareness of the now. The present moment is the only time that's real. It's constantly renewing itself, which allows us to renew ourselves. We are only ever one moment, one decision away from a fresh start. This simple yet profound shift in your awareness has the power to calm you down and, hopefully, allow you the space to choose an alternative way, so you win no matter what.

CHAPTER 9

THE GRASS ISN'T ALWAYS
GREENER

Live life and take chances. Believe that everything
happens for a reason and don't regret. Love to the
fullest and you will find true happiness in life. Realize
that things go wrong and people change, but things do
go on. Sometimes things weren't meant to be. What is
supposed to happen will work its way out.

—Oprah Winfrey

Our Life-Changing Decision

When I first met Declan, I discovered he had an intense passion for Australia. He had spent several months there, developed some great friendships, and loved the country. He loved it so much that we went there every other year on holiday over the next sixteen years. And on our last holiday there, something happened that changed our lives. Following a wonderful evening socializing with our friends, a conversation ensued that got everyone fired up as we were encouraged to move to Australia. There was great excitement as we were reminded of all the benefits of such a move. It was a bit like a commercial for the Aussie tourism board, but we were in on it too and needed little convincing of the beautiful lifestyle that potentially awaited us. The promise of a well-paid job and sponsorship made it very easy to consider.

At the time, back home, Declan was running a very successful business but was bored. He was ready for change and was keen to explore this opportunity in Australia, especially with the prospect of having a great job lined up. It was a massive decision to make, and we spent many early mornings over cups of tea at the kitchen table deliberating the pros and cons of such a move. Torn between leaving family, friends, and our comfortable lifestyle to start over in a new country was not an easy decision. The clock ticked, and with each tick, we were reminded of our chronological clock. We were fast approaching the cut-off age for application; we needed to act quickly.

Our inner Peter Pan and Pollyanna surfaced and sprinkled their optimism and sense of adventure on the project. And as I've mentioned before, I love adventure. Declan's enthusiasm and belief that we would be successful anywhere tipped the balance.

However, if I had a trickle of doubt, our son Finn, who was nine years old at the time, had a waterfall of apprehension.

He was unhappy to be leaving his friends and everything he knew to move to the other side of the world. We reassured him that he would have no trouble making friends and that it wouldn't be long before he would love it there. In effect, we projected our life experiences and expectations onto him. He didn't have much of a choice. Everyone around us was concerned. They thought we were mad and that we had to be undergoing a midlife crisis.

"Why are you selling the goose that lays the golden egg?" was a familiar question Declan was asked, referring to his thriving business. Friends and family asked other questions as they looked at us incredulously on more than one occasion:

"Why do you have to go to the other side of the world to live your life?"

"Isn't Ireland good enough for you?"

"What will you do if it doesn't work out?"

The doubts of others did nothing to deter us or make us rethink our plans. We made up our minds to go, although I very conveniently didn't discuss it outside of our home very often.

Going through the lengthy visa process took a while, but when the email arrived with news that we'd been successful, we looked skyward in gratitude and believed it was all going to plan. The angel cards and pendulum were offering positive vibes. While many of you might not allow such unusual means of corroboration to guide your life-changing decisions, they have been serving me well for many a year. Furthermore, a prediction of a move to Australia from a clairvoyant eighteen months previously, before we'd ever considered the move, offered more proof that we were meant to go.

We went through a frenzied clearing out of our home, selling things, giving things away, and finally, packing what we thought we needed. My usual nostalgic self frequently paused as it felt like we were packing away some of our most treasured memories in what was a loving and welcoming home. I can't lie; it was heartrending.

As I looked around and bubble-wrapped the many framed photos, tears rolled as I recalled the day we brought Finn home for the first time. It was cold and wet but perfect. Greeted by my doting mother, sister, and brother, he was welcomed into what we thought would be his forever home. Echoes of my brother's words of praise as we walked through the front door, "You did it, Poll," flooded my heart. I did it. I was a mother, my greatest wish, and I felt like the luckiest person in the world.

More happy memories surfaced as I emptied every room, thinking of the many guests who visited and left a little piece of themselves in the air. I'd miss the lengthy gatherings in the kitchen where we drank wine and ate delicious food, often prepared by one of our friends, satisfying our palates while we put the world to rights. Then, I recalled the excited chatter of Finn and his pals as they kicked a football for hours on end before crashing on the sofa in front of the TV with their favorite treats as they watched one show after another on the many sleepovers.

My yoga studio was such a special place for me. It had its own sounds over the years, as we "om'ed" and "aah'ed" our way through each class, always with a giggle and laugh, usually at my expense. The après-yoga chats were heartwarming in the main and occasionally caused a tear as the many clients who had become friends shared their joys and challenges.

Once I moved past the melancholy of it all, my attitude to making this next phase of our lives a success became my goal. So, we rented out our house with a plan to sell it at the first opportunity, fearing that not doing so would give us an easy get-out clause.

The farewells and goodbyes were painful. Great friends and family came together to send us on our merry way. The most challenging part was seeing my parents so inconsolable on the morning of our departure. I almost changed my mind. They looked so forlorn and confused; I could barely hold their gaze. I felt selfish, guilty, and full of regret. It was a woeful moment where I felt deeply that I had let them down.

As we took to the sky in our comfortable business class seats, the usual delight and exhilaration of travel escaped us. There was an indescribable feeling between us, expressed with long gazes, tightly held hands, and no sound. I closed my eyes and prayed we'd made the right decision. I knew I had to trust that we had. I also knew that if it didn't work out, there was a good reason and that we would find a way.

Perhaps our ten-day stopover in Bali would release the tension and prepare us for our new beginning.

Paradise Found?

Bali did not disappoint. Elephant rides, golf for the boys, and traditional Balinese massages for me kept us occupied. A trip to Ubud on the trail of Liz Gilbert to meet the famous Balinese medicine man Ketut Liyer was incredible. Even though we didn't meet him due to his deteriorating health, we had the pleasure of meeting his son who, interestingly, told me that our move to Australia would be short-lived.

Within two weeks of arriving in our newfound paradise, things went pear-shaped. Declan's job didn't materialize as expected, and it felt like we were on the back foot right from the start.

We had just rented a beautiful property on the beach in an expensive part of town. Finn was enrolled in the private school where our friend's children went. I was getting organized to build my coaching and yoga business, and Declan was learning a whole new industry in telecommunications. We both needed to work our magic if we were to make this choice a success.

Our main focus was on settling in and making sure that Finn was happy. There was no time for brooding; we needed to get moving and make it work. However, it wasn't long before I began to question myself and wondered if I had listened to my intuition or my ego. Doubt, worry, and anxiety were creeping up on me like the unwelcome cockroaches in my kitchen that simultaneously filled me with fear and disgust.

I had to stay focused and get my business off the ground. I was genuinely excited to start coaching and helping clients with my new skills. I hired a branding and marketing expert and got my website up and running. My new business was open, and I was ready and eager to work. Except, where were the clients? I was so green. I had so much to learn in this coaching space and online world. The adage, "When you fail to plan, it means that you are planning to fail" started to haunt me. Yikes! I realized that I hadn't got a clue what I was doing, and I didn't know which way to turn.

I thought I'd go back to reliable yoga teaching. After all, I had built a flourishing business back home with many happy clients. Surely, it would be the same here. I was convinced setting up my classes would be easy. The Gold Coast seemed like the perfect place. It was, and that was the problem. It was saturated to the point that some studios were closing down. Several refusals to teach at various yoga studios due to the already full timetables left me feeling crushed. I found a way eventually, even if it meant hiring a studio at 6 a.m. on a Saturday so that I would feel useful. I'll be forever grateful to the fabulous women who will never know how much their showing up meant to me.

Continuing to teach yoga was unsustainable as the numbers eventually dwindled for one reason or another. Competing with inexpensive gym memberships offering unlimited classes was challenging, not to mention the many free yoga classes on the beach.

I was demoralized, deflated, and worn out. Used to my persistence paying off, I found it tough as the harder I tried, the less it worked out.

So here I was, walking barefoot on the most idyllic beach every day, on the edge of the most spectacular ocean, inhaling the fresh air and sunshine, but feeling hopeless. I'd never felt this way ever before. I was used to working and earning a living. Here I was in unfamiliar territory, and I was petrified.

I was prepared to find a way even though it filled me with quiet trepidation. My days were spent networking, where I met some fantastic women while figuring out the coaching world. My confidence was plummeting, sleepless nights were increasing, and anxiety was advancing at lightning speed. I spent money on course after course to help troubleshoot my circumstances and on too many Thai massages to release the stress from my body and soul.

Internally, I was questioning almost everything about myself. Was my accent wrong? Was I lacking some critical skills? Was it clear what I could provide? How were we going to continue to afford this lifestyle? Our outgoings far exceeded our income, and the fees at Finn's private school and golf academies were proving to be excessive. Of course, there were alternatives that cost less, but we wanted to provide him with the best we could.

I was unquestionably being tested. Every day after I'd drop Finn at school, I'd go for a walk on the beach, plugged into some motivational talk or other on YouTube. God, I needed the inspiration to keep me going. I wanted to believe that things would improve for us, but I wasn't finding any evidence of that. Some days, I was on my knees begging God to direct me and show me the way. My distress was getting increasingly difficult to disguise. I was hiding it from my family in Ireland as the last thing I wanted was to upset and worry them. I tried to keep it from Finn, but that was more difficult to do as he saw me putting in the hours until late into the night. I said the bare minimum to our friends as I didn't want to come across as needy, but I was living a lie, and it was painful. I felt like a part of me was dying inside, and it was hard to breathe at times.

Getting a job wasn't an option. Despite my many careers and past experiences, I felt that I would only be able to get a minimum-wage job. We had no family to support us in looking after Finn, and quite frankly, I didn't see the point in working just to hand over my wages to a childminder.

I had always been able to turn things around fast and been proactive in improving my circumstances. From a young age, I'd earned money to pay for whatever I wanted. I applied for jobs and always got them. I was used to getting what I wanted and might have taken it for granted. However, this time, I was a mature, experienced woman but felt trapped. I didn't know where to turn. It was only when I turned inward that I was able to keep going because deep down, I'm a believer, and I knew instinctively that when one door closes, another one opens. I was waiting impatiently.

Despite the situation, I met and made friends for life. Nonetheless, I felt hopelessly rejected. Nothing seemed to be working. As time went on, I felt alone, like I did when living in London, even though I had my husband and son this time. The game was up. To quote a friend of mine, "I felt as useful as a chocolate teapot," a complete waste of space. What did I have to offer? Who was I kidding? The inner critic's voice was loud and menacing, and I found it hard to look in the mirror.

A memory surfaced of a day I was walking with a friend in the woods back home in Ireland. At the time, my life was in bliss mode. I was happily teaching yoga and running my holistic healing center. As we walked and chatted, I felt called to share one of the seven spiritual laws of yoga principles I'd been teaching. It was to do with the law of detachment, and the message was about being able to embrace uncertainty in life and learn to be blissfully free from attachment to the outcome. It reminds us not to force solutions but to allow them to surface spontaneously. Written by my mentor, Deepak Chopra, I absorbed every word into my being. However, for some reason, on this occasion, I found myself saying to my friend that I understood this theoretically and that sometimes it's easy to glaze over such wisdom when things are going well in life. But I hoped that I would adopt this principle should I ever be faced with a major challenge. As a teacher, walking the talk has always been important to me.

Well, as life would have it, here I was, faced with such an opportunity to test my case. Loyalty to my soul was supreme, but so, too, was my duty to my family. I barely talked to Declan about these doubts. Instead, I reinforced the view that things were soon going to turn around. I would often say, "Today is the day!" There had to be a way.

Declan is an eternal optimist and is always so supportive and encouraging. However, he was concerned about my well-being, especially with my two bouts of shingles within a few months of one another. He knew my history as a worker bee and my longing to share what I loved. When we'd have time alone together, we'd reflect on how this move was affecting Finn.

We often welled up when we recalled the day he was learning to use a boogie board at Nippers, the junior branch of the life-saving surf club on the beach where we lived. This was a social event for parents and kids. It was an early start every Sunday morning, and Declan couldn't wait to get Finn going.

So, just a few short weeks after we arrived there, Finn stood in line awaiting his turn to brave the waves of the Pacific Ocean on a boogie board. He knew no one. My heart was aching for him. He looked so out of place, pale by comparison to the tanned bodies all around him, but mostly he looked sad, uncertain, and lonely. He was missing his pals. It was such a deep contrast to the hundreds of kids who were calling one another's names and high-fiving, a reflection of their established friendships and sportsmanship. Still, my little trooper put on a brave face, not wanting to admit to us that he didn't want to participate.

The next thing we knew, one of the club's senior members accompanied him right out into the ocean. Declan and I stood by, cheering him on like two excited teenagers. We both wanted this to be one of his best experiences, a chance to feel part of the local community and make new friends. Instead, Finn came off the board, and he banged himself hard in the chest, winding him and causing him to swallow a gallon of water. Awkward and embarrassed, he plowed on, again not wanting to make a fuss. We were proud of his tenacity and resilience and knew it would stand him in good stead in his life. But for now, we had to take care of the bruising in his chest and severe pain. We soon became acquainted with the local physiotherapist and chiropractor.

It wasn't until several weeks later when I lay beside him before he went to sleep one night that I put my hand on the area where this pain was persisting, and the floodgates of emotion erupted. I had suggested that I'd do some reiki on the area, and that was when my beautiful boy began to wobble and sob. He'd been holding on to so much sadness and anxiety. His heart ached, and no amount of physiotherapy or chiropractic adjusting could have released that. In between the blubbering and bawling, he shared that he was missing everyone back home and that we should never have moved there. Little did he know that I was feeling the same way, but I didn't want to admit that to him as I knew we had invested so much into this move, and I was still holding on to the idea that it had to work out for us. Declan came upstairs to say goodnight to Finn, only to find us both wrapped around one another, bawling. Then we were three blubbering messes in the bed.

Things gradually improved for Finn, and he made some great friends and golfed several times a week, competing and even getting to meet some of the pro golfers at various championships. He got to taste different food and loved the sushi restaurants. He even learned some Japanese.

He went to school where our friend's children went. They had a very different curriculum structure from home. He thrived in that learning environment and loved his teachers. Things were looking up for him until he got bullied about playing golf and being Irish. The Gold Coast is all about the surf. Kids grow up in the sea; it's second nature to them. Golfing was something that they saw their dad or granddad do and wasn't seen as a young person's sport. We dealt swiftly with the incident and resolved it amicably, but it was now just another peg on the line of things that made us rethink our decision.

As time passed, we were running out of money and hope, and it was terrifying. The substantial fund we had taken to Australia had been subsidizing our lifestyle and was now almost depleted. Then one event almost broke me. It was mid-December 2016. We owned and needed two cars, and both were due for renewal of insurance and tax. We couldn't afford to pay the money due on both cars for a minimum of six months, so I had to go to the local government office and request another payment option.

I will never forget that day as long as I live. In true Gold Coast style, the sun shone its brilliance, and the clear blue sky above created a perfect canopy on this not-so-perfect day. As I drove to the office, I felt ashamed and like a failure. Looking around at the other drivers on the road, I wondered what was going on in their lives. Of course, I knew there were many people less fortunate than I was, but that day, I felt very sorry for myself and wanted the world to stop just for a moment and for someone to hold my hand and tell me that this was all a big joke.

"Well now, Miss Yoga, meditating spiritual teacher, believer of miracles," said the sarcastic voice in my head, "How's this for uncertainty? How are you going to handle this? It doesn't seem like you're too detached from the outcome, Miss Know-It-All."

But something inside surfaced that made me walk with renewed dignity into the expansive open-plan office, where I collected my ticket and waited to be summoned. I scanned the space for others in the same position as me. They were oblivious to my presence, and that old, haunting loneliness returned. Eventually, I was called, and I sat down apprehensively. There was no privacy between the booths, and I felt very vulnerable and exposed before I even opened my mouth. I placed the forms on the counter, and the woman who was attending to me never raised her head to greet me but kept her eyes on the paper in front of her.

"So, you can't pay both these balances right now?" she asked with eyes firmly glued to her desk.

"That's right," I said. "My husband needs one car for work, and I need one to take my son to and from school."

With her eyes still stubbornly looking downwards, the following words that came out of her mouth cut me to the bone: "So, you're in hardship?" What? Hardship? Did I hear her right? Much as I had wanted the world to stop earlier, as I processed what she had just said, I felt as if I were part of a slow-motion scene in a movie. The word penetrated my very soul. I had hardly ever heard that word before, and indeed it had never applied to me. It is said to have pride is foolish. I have to agree. Any feeling of self-respect was disappearing as I had to face the truth of some bad choices we'd made. That critical voice chimed in again just to make sure I was getting it. "Ha, Miss Perfect, not so perfect now, are you? You're in a right mess, aren't you?" It woke me up.

I sat up in my seat and leaned in a bit closer, not wanting the other customers to hear me. "Excuse me," I said, "I would like you to look at me. I want you to see me and listen to me, please." My voice was quivering as I explained how my husband had to drive to the outback almost daily to sell a product very few wanted while having to meet his targets or face being let go. Holding back the tears, I asked her if she had any idea how hard it was for me to sit opposite her and have to ask for this kind of help. I wanted to be seen for who I was, honest, hardworking, optimistic, kind, and loving— someone who was experiencing an unfamiliar situation and was terrified. I wasn't a criminal, but I felt like an outcast, and little did this woman know that her behavior towards me was the last straw. Just a few minutes before entering this building, I had bought our Christmas tree in the nearby charity shop. Something was wrong in our world right then, and I felt humiliated, inadequate, and afraid.

You could say that I got her attention. She stood up, and I noticed tears in her eyes. She excused herself, and when she returned, she thanked me for drawing her attention to me. I can only surmise that I interrupted her from a routine operation that had become mechanical, perhaps desensitizing her for her protection. And while still clearly emotional, she stamped the form, allowing me to pay for just three months on both cars. Hardship? The word played over and over in my mind. Here we were living beside the beach in paradise but probably not for much longer.

I vowed I would never be in such circumstances again. When I got to my car, I sat and cried, not just for myself, but for every person who has found themselves in a similar situation, feeling judged, ignored, dismissed, and disregarded. The subsequent call to Declan was infused with absolute determination to use this painful life experience as fuel to get our act together once and for all.

Something Must Be Wrong with Me

I had so many contrasting experiences and emotions during the first few months of 2017. We had survived Christmas, and Finn got his usual gifts thanks to a loan from a friend. Despite the humiliation and unlikelihood of things improving for us, I was extremely aware of the abundance all around me. We may have been getting poor in paradise, but there was still an inner knowing that something good would come of this.

As an early riser, one of my favorite things to do was greet the day at sunrise, and I needed it. It gave me hope and a sense of peace. To observe the morning sky fill with the most stunning display of its creative ability was genuinely breathtaking and kept me connected to God. I never took for granted, not for a second, that I was part of this spectacle and that I was being shown that despite life's ups and downs, the sun would continue to rise, and a new day would dawn. Everything that I had learned from my meditation and yoga studies came to my aid. It wasn't just a theoretical practice but a meaningful tool. The "someday I might need this knowledge" had arrived, and I was calling it up with a sense of urgency.

On those early morning beach walks, I was entertained by the enthusiasm of the eager surfers as they ran towards the ocean to catch a wave and ride it back to shore. I both admired and envied their sense of freedom. They came from all over the world and had one thing in common, an inspiring fearlessness. I watched, intrigued, but knew that I wasn't ever going to join them.

I felt safer walking on the soft, white sand, planning and plotting my next steps. My morning mantra had become, "Just trust; it's all unfolding perfectly."

Some days, I was able to maintain belief in that promise, but on other days, I found myself saying, "There must be something wrong with me." I knew I had to find that fearlessness within again.

Deep down, I seriously doubted myself. I felt invisible and utterly purposeless. I was so used to getting what I wanted, even if it meant working two or three jobs. I found myself feeling resentful of the strangers around me who had a purpose and made a difference with their work.

When I worked for British Airways, I was assisting a female passenger with her luggage in the business class cabin when she looked me straight in the eye as I placed her bag in the overhead locker and said, "I bet you wish you'd worked a little harder in school." Even though I could have been offended at the time, I wasn't. I simply looked at this woman, who felt superior to me, in disbelief. I thought to myself, "How can she be so judgmental? She knows nothing about me." I think due to my ongoing search for meaning and purpose I felt something was brewing for me, which allowed me to feel unfazed. However, back in Australia, I wondered what my life would be like if I had worked harder in school. I certainly couldn't imagine my unlimited potential. I knew I was being tested and had to trust that my potential was there, buried beneath the doubts and ideas I held about how things should be. I just couldn't tap into it or find the right channel to move it through, and it was soul-destroying.

So, from this desperate challenge came an excellent and critical insight. I naturally started to question everything. I recognized that I had become complacent with my self-care practices and the deeper connection to my spirit in all my doing. I had forgotten to just be. I had stopped checking in on myself and, in my darker moments, saw myself as a true enemy of my soul, a failure to my family, purpose, and life's mission.

As I became more compassionate towards myself, I knew that I wasn't a failure because I hadn't quit. I was still hanging in there, if even by a thread, enough to hold on to the idea that I was being led. All I had to do was trust. This was the one constant instruction I followed, and it gave me the confidence to continue.

We all need help at some point, and that includes me. I never had an issue with anyone else needing help before and would be among the first to help if I could. But when it came to me, needing help made me feel weak and therefore vulnerable, so I rarely asked for it.

That thinking was soon changed thanks to the author and researcher Brené Brown. Her book *Daring Greatly* gave me the strength to be honest with myself during those bleaker moments of despair and self-loathing.

My father's words to me when I was that enthusiastic and impulsive teen came flooding into my mind. He would look at me and caution that faraway fields were not always greener. I wasn't sure what that meant at the time, and any attempt he made to explain it to me to prevent me from doing something he might think foolish or dangerous fell on deaf ears. I seemed to have an attitude of "That doesn't apply to me." Little did I know.

Treasure in Your Own Backyard

It wasn't until recently that I heard a story that explains his point very well. Told by the late American author Earl Nightingale, the story details how an African farmer heard that people were making millions by discovering diamond mines. He decided to join the search and sold his farm. However, his search was futile, and he threw himself into a river and drowned.

In a twist of fate, the man who had bought his farm found an unusual stone in a stream on the property. It turned out this stone was a diamond of great value, and he discovered more just like them all over the farm. It became one of the richest diamond mines in the world.

The moral of the story is that the first farmer had been sitting on a fortune but hadn't taken the time to learn what diamonds look like in their rough state. Similarly, each of us is standing on our own acres of diamonds if we'd only look a little closer. But many of us run away to what we think are better places or greener pastures, only to discover that life isn't as we had hoped it to be.

This story reminds me also of how ignorant we are about ourselves. We are like diamonds in the rough, requiring some polishing in the form of personal development to awaken our true potential to become all that we can be. We each have so many gifts locked up within us. Our job is to unlock and refine them until they become the gems that reflect who we are.

We took a chance and learned a lesson or two in moving to Australia, and I'm grateful for it. Our backyard was always good enough, but we got caught up in the promise of adventure and pastures new. The harsh truth is that we didn't appreciate what we had. I can't turn the clock back, but I can hit the pause button more often to make more conscious choices.

I didn't believe in myself enough in Australia. We moved to a new country, and at the same time, I was starting a new business. I know people who have done this very successfully, and knowing that only added to my feeling of inadequacy.

On reflection, the move didn't work out for many reasons. Probably top of the list was that we had a safety net; we hadn't sold our home, so the door was still open. It was a plan B mentality, which isn't usually how I do things. I typically approach my goals and dreams with an attitude of "It's going to work out, there's no going back, no matter what."

Wherever You Go, You'll Take Yourself

Another sage piece of advice from my father was, "Wherever you go, you'll take yourself with you." This saying has enlightened me, especially regarding my work. It implies that no matter where you are or where you go, and no matter what you do, nothing will change if your thinking does not. Our thoughts go everywhere with us, and what you believe in will end up giving you the results that you think about. I always wanted a big, happy life, and I realize my dad's words of caution were meant to encourage me to cultivate a more profound sense of myself so I could learn that true happiness comes from within. I didn't listen; I had to find out for myself, and that's okay. It's been costly at times, but it has also been worth it as it has all been part of my journey. I often joke that I'm like a cat with nine lives. I believe that I've had someone watching over me my whole life because I could have had some very different outcomes otherwise.

Hindsight is a great teacher, and I consider myself to be a good student. I have analyzed my behavior and way of thinking. Unlike the unfortunate African farmer I described earlier, I feel blessed to have had the wherewithal and courage to keep going and count my losses as blessings. I didn't indulge in a pity party for long; no party is a good party with only one guest. Victimhood was not a place in which I wanted to live. Every moment offered me the chance to think better, feel better, and do better. That was my focus. If the rocket can fail on its way to the moon, I can fail to get to where I want to go. Something much greater than I could ever imagine for myself was up ahead.

CHAPTER 10

BROKE BUT NOT BROKEN

*No doubt the reason is that character cannot
be developed in ease and quiet. Only through
experience of trial and suffering can the soul
be strengthened, vision cleared, ambition inspired,
and success achieved.*

—Helen Keller

Rebuilding Our Lives—The Bounce Back

In May 2017, I was awakened at 4 a.m. one morning and heard a voice whispering to me: "It's time." I elbowed Declan and excitedly told him, "We're going home." Further discussion was unnecessary; we both knew to trust this explicit instruction, and nineteen days later, we were back in Ireland.

Saying an emotional farewell to new and old friends who made us so welcome was not easy. But, alas, even they had to concede that staying any longer was not an option.

Going home filled us with some trepidation but mostly exhilaration. We had so much to do and so much to consider. But that could all wait until we were reunited with our family and friends. First, we had the arduous task of packing up, organizing the transportation, and finalizing things with Declan's employers and Finn's school. We also had to notify the agency overseeing our home's rental about our decision to return and give the tenant adequate notice.

The anguish had lifted, and my morning beach walks took on a new rhythm, a somewhat faster pace as my hurried feet left behind footprints of a woman on a mission. And just as quickly as the sea swallowed up the evidence of my presence there each morning, we were home in Ireland again.

The greeting at Dublin airport was a mixture of tears, hugs, and laugh-out-loud moments. I held my mother in my arms and leaned back a little, holding her gaze in absolute silence. It seemed as if time stood still, allowing us to acknowledge one another. My unspoken words that wafted through the ether from my mind to hers were, "I'm sorry I made you sad and worried. Please forgive me." The softness and twinkle in my mother's eyes spoke volumes. Her expression at that moment will always stay with me. Despite the hustle and bustle around us, I knew that my mother telepathically communicated to me, "You're home, that's all that matters now, and no one will ever tell you, 'I told you so.' Relax, everything is going to be okay." That silent exchange was all the encouragement I needed.

It seems crazy when I think of it because we'd been away for just under two years and had been home twice on holidays during that time, but the sound of Ireland was music to my ears. I found myself listening more intensely to the accents and colloquialisms I had grown up with, where swear words add theatre and flair to the story being told. We knew we were home. It was where I needed to be. Another memory surfaced that depicts this point. In 2009, I was training to be a yoga teacher at the Chopra Center in the La Costa Resort. Overjoyed with the experience, the southern Californian vibes, and Deepak on tap, I excitedly told one of the Chopra goddesses I wanted to work there. We were in line waiting for coffee when she turned around and politely said that I needed to do this work in Ireland. At that moment, I knew she was right, and bringing both yoga and meditation to my community has been both a blessing and a gift ever since. There's no doubt that while I am a globetrotter, Ireland is where I most belong.

Our Relationship Becomes Stronger

When we came back from Australia, we were broke, but we were not broken. We had an inner drive and an awareness that this had all happened for us, and this gift was becoming more apparent as each day passed.

It would be a lie to say that we didn't feel aggrieved by what at times felt like an unwise move, and I think it's fair to say that not every marriage would have survived.

However, ours grew more robust, and we respected one another more for the efforts we were both making to reclaim a level of comfort and stability in our lives. We opened the miracle toolbox and started to do the work. We both knew that we had to dig deep to get back to where we were financially before our move. We wrote our goals on whiteboards and hung them proudly in our home office. We meditated, prayed, and maybe occasionally begged God to accelerate the process. We practiced the Hawaiian forgiveness prayer and stuck the message on sticky notepaper all over the house. "I'm sorry, please forgive me, thank you, I love you," became a mantra we both sometimes chanted in unison. I believe it helped us both to release blame and shame, let go of the pain, and embrace the enormity of the task ahead.

We set out to maintain a sense of awe about the true joys of life, the magnificence of nature, and the ability to see the best in people and our circumstances. We had a deeper appreciation of everything as if we were seeing things for the first time. I was reminded of a quote by Marcel Proust, "The real voyage of discovery consists not in seeking new landscapes but in having new eyes."

We knew we had to build a stronger foundation. We were starting over, but not as novices. I've since realized that we were both programmed for success, and part of every successful journey are the failures, mistakes, and losses. We always expected great things to happen, and they did. Even heart-wrenching challenges became something to commemorate. This time, we were bringing our life experiences and lessons learned to the kitchen table, where we planned out our next moves with many a cup of tea and coffee.

A New Respect for Money

To help us feel at home again, we set about cleaning up our house. In the past, we would have hired professionals to paint our home and tidy up our garden; Declan took on these jobs with enthusiasm. One thing that bothered us about living in Australia was that we had been tenants and had to ask for permission to hang a picture or move a nail. Now back in our own home, we had total freedom, and it felt so good.

Having to be cautious about what we were spending our money on made us feel childlike and grateful for what we had. We turned any disagreement around fast and laughed more at ourselves. If we said it once, we said it a hundred times, "Thank you, God, for our health; our health is our wealth." As long as we remained healthy, we knew we had a big chance to bounce back and move ahead.

I knew that our somewhat naïve attitude towards spending money and the reasons we had never properly addressed it had required some attention for quite a while. And just like that, the lesson we both needed to learn about money took us around the world on a costly but worthwhile ride.

Our attitude to spending was reflected in a "Sure, we could be dead tomorrow" or "You only live once" way of thinking, and that was usually enough coaxing required to book yet another luxury holiday or change the car. We were as good as each other at earning and spending money. My late father-in-law expressed concern about our spending ability when we announced our engagement after just five months of dating. He said our relationship would never work out as we were both big spenders. He was right that we were big spenders, but his predictions otherwise were wrong. Just over twenty-five years later, at the time of writing, we're still here taking the rough with the smooth, and we're all the happier for it.

For as long as we had been together, we had enjoyed an excellent standard of living. We went on several five-star holidays every year; we dined out a lot, upgraded our cars, and had more clothes and comforts than we needed. Yet, we didn't miss any of that while we rebuilt our lives. Those things are nice to have and do, and I've never been shy to say that I enjoy a bit of luxury. Nothing is as important as the people you love, and material possessions can never replace that. They're simply symbols, an effect of our hard work and the choices we make. However, they will never guarantee happiness or joy, and we had many a chance to prove that point to ourselves.

I've always had an internal battle with wanting to live a simple, spiritual life while enjoying the abundance that life has to offer. Once, when I doubted continuing my career in the guards and ended yet another relationship, I considered joining an enclosed order of nuns. You might say that religious life is the opposite of what I've been sharing—it is—but I wanted to escape. I was exhausted with my life choices at the time, and I admit that I was looking for an easy way out. I felt that this would be the answer. At least, it would probably have pleased my dad. So, I walked into a church, found a priest, and asked him what the procedure was. With a raised eyebrow and a scornful look, he inquired as to whether I had recently ended a relationship. When I admitted that I had, he immediately suggested I wait three months and that if I still felt the same way, he would happily introduce me to the Reverend Mother in the parish. I did not return, and the notion wore off within days. My mother reacted with a smirk, "A nun where there's *none* wanted."

Renewing Our Purpose

Like a wild bear who had come out of hibernation, hungry for something to eat, I was a famished woman eager to fill her emptiness and purposelessness with something big, juicy, and fulfilling. So, landing back in Dublin in June 2017, we knew our priority was to keep the roof over our heads and roll up our sleeves. However, with the limited cash available to us, we had only enough to buy a cheap car and make some necessary home improvements.

I cannot write this story without mentioning the love and support from our family and friends from both an emotional and a financial perspective. Neither of us had an income when we came home, and the only way we could justify borrowing from family and friends was to make a mindset shift around it and suggest that they invest in us, and we would pay them back with interest. Somehow, it helped us maintain some dignity and self-respect. I borrowed from one of my brothers, who, without any hesitation, gave me what I needed and made me cry when he said, "I believe in you, Pauline; I know you'll make it again." It meant so much to have had that support and faith in me.

We will be eternally grateful for the kindness and lack of judgment shown to us. You'll know who your real friends are when the going is tough, and ours did not let us down.

Nevertheless, asking for help was not something that Declan and I enjoyed. He has been working since the age of eight in his family jewelry business. It was a typical family business dynamic where there was no choice but to get involved and help, whether you wanted to or not.

He showed his entrepreneurial tendencies from a very young age when he became acquainted with some of the local winos who would leave their empty cider and beer bottles in a bus shelter for him. They would often throw a stone at his bedroom window in the early hours of the morning as they stumbled home, alerting him to where they'd left the latest stash.

Young Declan would throw his clothes over his pajamas, head off to collect the said stash, and relocate it to his wardrobe. In this covert operation, he returned the valuable bottles to the shop and received a few meager coins in return.

While I had a very different upbringing from my husband, I share his work ethic. The good life always appealed to me, and I was forever prepared to get it for myself. I've already mentioned my eagerness to get a job and go to Italy with my school when I was thirteen. (Although earlier, I didn't say that the Italian boys motivated me to save my well-earned wages more than *il Papa* and the Sistine Chapel). Luckily, that same drive to thrive exists today, so that's why I felt like such a failure when I was *not* working in Australia.

We shared our successes generously with family and friends over the years. I think that's why everyone was so open to helping us in our darkest hour. The law of karma was proving itself: what you put out, you get back. So, hallelujah, we were going to get through this most challenging time in our lives.

The raw memories of the lonely days in Australia would surface occasionally. Still, my vision for the future helped me to physically get up every day to tell a new story. That same vision filled me with the hope that we'd been given more than a second chance but an opportunity to do better.

Driven by the desire and an urgent need to rebuild our lives, I knew I had to use my recent experiences and feeling of rejection in an empowering way. I had been accustomed to getting what I wanted in life for the most part, even if it took some time. Therefore, I was like a dog with a bone when it came to my goals and dreams—relentless, maybe stubborn. I think I've proven that with my story of motherhood.

As I intimated earlier, I learned something fundamental when reflecting on my relatively short time in Australia: *you don't get what you want, you get who you are and what you expect.* I finally had to admit that I went there expecting to be perceived as not good enough, and I let that idea in. New to coaching, I felt I wasn't experienced enough professionally, yet I'd spent most of my life doing it in one form or another. I compared myself with those whom I believed were better than I was. I realized I had done that at different stages of my life. At drama classes as a child, I wanted to be picked for the leading role but never expected to be as I felt inferior to the prettier, livelier girls. How little we value ourselves. One of my biggest regrets was when I held myself back from winning the 200 m sprint because it meant my best friend would have come in second.

It was a long time coming, but my dharma, my true purpose, was being revealed to me. That old way of thinking was never going to support my dreams. Over the last five years, at the time of writing, I have retrained myself to think differently to support who I am meant to be and to love that I'm helping so many others do the same. There's nothing quite like a contrast to show you the gap between where you are in your life and where you want to be. Don't you just love those lightbulb moments? The more you know what you don't want, the closer you are to discovering what you do want.

Remember what Steve Jobs said, "You can't connect the dots looking forward; you can only connect them looking backwards." I had so much time to look back and see how the writing was always on the wall about all my frantic trips to holistic fairs and markets, where I'd eagerly book sessions with shamans, healers, card readers, and clairvoyants, beseeching them to help me uncover my true purpose. A common theme ran through their psychic messages suggesting that I was a spiritual teacher with a gift of healing, something I got from my Nanny. I always felt a deep resonance with their predictions and wanted them to be true, but I had no clue how or when they would become apparent. It's comical when I think about how I've had feathers waved under my nose, drums beaten in my face, incense circled around my auric field, with healers chanting and clapping over my body as I lay in a trance-like state. Probably my favorite of all was standing in the River Ganges in Rishikesh getting a blessing from none other than a hotelier acting as a guru reciting some Hindu prayer in my direction. I did, however, sit at the feet of a modern-day guru and receive his blessing too. Guruji was a highly recognized mystic and a friend of my Indian friends. I was the only Westerner at the home where he led his teachings in New Delhi, but I felt like I belonged. India is a special place for me, and I deeply connect with its people and traditions.

I have been a seeker my whole life and open to anything that would accelerate my awakening and awareness. However, the time comes when you have to slow the external search down, turn your attention inward, and realize that no one can do it for you and no one is coming to save you either—this is your own role and responsibility. Wouldn't it be easy if a magic pill or something existed to do the heavy lifting for us? There is no such thing, and that's why the sooner you and I become accountable for ourselves, the sooner we can be living that bigger, better life. I believe that we all can receive guidance from our soul and become a messenger to others once we've demonstrated and validated this powerful communication in our own lives.

I also believe that some of the greatest healers and therapists have walked their own path of pain and therefore can have the empathy and understanding necessary to help us advance our dreams and goals. I'm reminded of some of the very ignorant assumptions I've heard over the years about therapy from people who needed it most. They were pointed in the direction of the therapists' past personal challenges as if to suggest, "How could someone who was messed up help me?" We probably all could benefit from therapy in our lives at some point, and I'd rather speak to someone who has done whatever it took to overcome their struggles than be treated from a theoretical perspective by someone else.

The most definitive therapy for me is honesty, admitting when I'm wrong, or at least not always right, and freely apologizing. Throughout history, families have held too many secrets. Hiding things to avoid being shamed or judged has done more harm to the individuals involved than if they had dared to speak up and if they had shared their burdens. Being honest with others without fear of disapproval or rejection is very therapeutic. While I know it takes some guts and confidence, it is liberating and empowering for all concerned. Isn't much of our suffering caused by doing things we don't want to do, putting up with things we don't enjoy, and allowing others to dominate us? Therefore, speak your truth. Do what's in your heart. Challenge the status quo.

Change the rules. You don't have to do what other people tell you to do, especially if you don't want to. As I tell all my clients, "no" is a complete sentence—it is a final answer. Nipping things in the bud and settling them on the spot is something we can choose to do. Trust your innate wisdom; I know you can access it. It knows the way.

When the Student Is Ready, the Teacher Appears

I've always loved the expression, "When the student is ready, the teacher appears." The teacher in question on this occasion, was Marisa Peer, a celebrity hypnotherapist and the creator of Rapid Transformational Therapy. I found her on YouTube on one of my many searches to find a way to believe in myself again during our time in Australia. She became synonymous with the affirmation "I am enough," and I quickly adopted it as my own.

Within ten days of returning home, I was off to London to attend a training with Marisa that moved me up the next rung on the ladder of my divine assignment.

I loved how this therapy offered a speedy solution to emotional pain. I was experiencing emotional distress at the time, and I didn't want it to last forever. Whilst many would argue that it takes years to heal from trauma and sadness, I saw firsthand how this approach focused on uprooting the cause of an emotional pattern and offered a new perspective to the client. I learned that no one should forever have to endure the negativity and limitation caused by false beliefs about oneself. I saw how this therapy would fit together with my energy work, coaching, and yoga background. I knew that I could help people in a genuinely holistic way. Understanding the power of the mind and its influence over all our results excited me. From the first time I began training as a holistic practitioner in 2001, empowering others fast was my main objective. Just as I didn't want to suffer long-term, I didn't want that for others either.

I became passionate about helping heal those who were robbed of the freedom to be who they were born to be based on their false beliefs about themselves. While growing up, many of us were not told that we had a purpose or that it was acceptable to try different things a number of times before we go on to find the things in life that are best suited to us and that give us the greatest joy. Sadly, all too many were told that they were useless and would never amount to anything of consequence.

Many of us didn't know that we could let go of the past, and instead continue living in a mental prison shackled to every negative experience we've had, marking time daily while unconsciously attracting more of the same. Nobody warned us that first, we make our beliefs, and then our beliefs make us.

Living in ignorance of the power of our potential and the possibilities for our lives is my idea of hell on earth. If this sounds like you, it's not your fault. You may have never been told about your value or worth or been encouraged to follow your heart. Maybe you were not praised for your efforts and gifts and were criticized when you did the things you were good at. You most likely had role models who were not told these things either.

You may have been punished for your honesty and had your apologies disregarded. You may have felt confused and afraid, left to figure things out on your own.

Ready to Serve

Two months after our return home, I finally opened my hypnotherapy practice. I was ready to serve in a new way. My enthusiastic, multitasking DIY husband had freshly painted my therapy room and yoga studio, and my wonderful mother surprised me with brand-new yoga mats. Now all I had to do was wait. Before long, the classes were full, and the happy, familiar faces of my loyal clients I had grown to love and call friends were filling up the mats in the studio. They came with flowers, cards, framed pictures, and of course, chocolates. Tears were intermingled with many laughs, bear hugs, and enthusiastic expressions of yoga.

I had turned the corner. I felt useful. I had meaningful and valued work to do again. Things were looking up.

CHAPTER 11

THE MISSING PIECES

Self-trust is the first secret of success.

—Ralph Waldo Emerson

Pursuing my purpose didn't end with opening the studio; it was just beginning. There I was, loved up on teaching yoga and hypnotizing clients towards emotional freedom when the perpetual student within me wanted more knowledge to support my work. That childhood message, *there is another way*, was making increasingly more sense to me the more I continued with the inner work. I could see that there was another way for me to work with people that allowed me to show them that there was another way for them to live beyond fear and to alchemize their low self-esteem into high self-love. I saw myself in the ideal position to demonstrate that it's never too late to make a change. I envisioned helping people to reclaim their power from the past and be free to start their lives over. I continue to do that, and it's the very best feeling in the world. From my therapy room in the corner of a village in the west of Ireland, I have reached people worldwide to help them see that they always have a choice to view their past from a different perspective and to start over.

My fascination with the mind also began to assert itself. I wanted to share how collectively we've been hypnotized to think, feel, and behave in a limiting way via the media, our governments, the church, advertising, and our conditioning. More than anything, I wanted people to know that they had the power within to dehypnotize themselves from false beliefs and propaganda designed to divide us and make us think that we could never succeed.

Say Yes to Happiness

The one common theme that I began to notice from each client was a desire to be happy and to find inner peace. While the yogis enjoyed the classes and the hypnotherapy clients were relieved to start life anew, sometimes the happiness disappeared when they were faced with the day-to-day demands and problems that life dished out. I wanted to know more about the meaning of the saying, "Happiness is an inside job" so that I could teach it and embody it in my own life. This led me to train as a happiness trainer with the fabulous Marci Shimoff, who wrote the well-researched book on the subject, *Happy for No Reason*.

I took my signature Say Yes to Happiness seminar around Ireland. It was uplifting and brought many laughs and lightbulb moments to the attendees. It showed how much power we have to alter our thinking and ultimately increase our joy. I shared the message in magazines and on radio, podcasts, and TV. I brought it into institutions and virtual classrooms, all the while reinforcing its message in my own home and heart.

One of the great lessons I share is around the great big myth of happiness. The problem for so many of us is that we think we'll be happy when we get a new car, go on holiday, win the lottery, get promoted, start a business, get married, have a family, and so the list continues. While all these things can temporarily make us happy, we fail to realize that while we are in wait mode, we are not allowing ourselves to be happy in the moment. Therefore, we are missing the real opportunity to experience true happiness, irrespective of our circumstances. We base our happiness on externals, thus giving away control over it.

What happens when our relationship ends, or we lose a job, a business, or a loved one? What happens to our happiness now? The truth is, that circumstances change all the time for everyone. Change is inevitable; how we respond to change is a choice. Our jobs, businesses, home, health, wealth, and love can disappear or end overnight, and I know how that feels. When we identify with those things and rely upon them for our joy, we can be left feeling lost and broken without them. Many live in a state of terror and high alert, waiting for the next blow to their sense of self. Allowing the outside world to be the source of our happiness is a reckless way to live, and long-term, it costs us dearly.

We've got it all wrong. According to Marci's extensive research, there's such a thing as a happiness set-point. Your circumstances affect only 10 percent of your happiness level, yet this is what we are always trying to change. Our DNA determines 50 percent of our happiness. It appears we are born either dreary or cheery. Which one are you? The best bit of the research indicates that our beliefs and habits determine the remaining 40 percent of our happiness set-point. Our thinking causes our beliefs and habits, and here's the enlightening news: we can change our thinking, our beliefs, and our habits, and in so doing, according to the study of epigenetics, we can influence our DNA by thinking and acting differently.

We can learn from this that the main difference between happy and unhappy people is their attitude and habits.

We all get tested from time to time to see if we're paying attention to what we're learning and if we're applying it. That's when knowledge is power. Learn, adapt, and apply. Even though I was born with a cheery disposition, I have been unhappy at times, and I have shared some of those times with you in this book. But the more I taught this material, the happier I became as I let go of some habits that were no longer serving me and cultivated new ones that supported the changes I wanted to make in my life. The one habit I am most proud of is not including alcohol in my life any longer, although I made this choice several years before I learned about happiness habits. I shared earlier in the book about not enjoying alcohol when I was a young Garda. However,

I became quite an accomplished drinker over the years, reveling in the early morning on many occasions. When our weekends were beginning on a Wednesday evening, I got the soul-filled nudge to change direction. I was completely off track from my values and what was important to me concerning my work and, most importantly, my role as a parent. My father didn't drink, and my mother had an odd one at a function. I never appreciated their abstinence when I was growing up and often wished my dad would get drunk and do funny things like I saw so many of my friends' dads do. Back then, I classified him as strict and boring, but as I got older, I was envious of my dad's discipline and sobriety and wanted so badly to be like him in this regard.

While I wasn't addicted to or dependent on alcohol, I saw how easy it was just to open a bottle of red and have a glass or three when we'd sit down after Finn was in bed. I began to despise myself. I felt weak. I particularly berated myself when I smoked a secret cigarette in the back garden, a much-loathed habit formed out of what I recognized as self-punishment. Inside, I wanted to be better and do better. I wanted a healthier life and to prove that I could stop doing something that made me feel like an imposter. It took me nearly thirty years to say a final no to drinking. I decided eight years ago to once and for all knock this out-of-date habit on the head as I wanted my son to see that you can enjoy your life without booze. Of course, he can choose for himself when he's older. I wanted him to be aware of his power of choice, and we have discussed this openly, among many other subjects. I am certainly far happier to be free of the trappings of drinking for no good reason, and so is my husband. He joined me four years later, having come to a similar realization.

Getting up before 6 a.m. is a habit that makes me happy. Many consider this the middle of the night, but I love the early morning. I can easily get up at 4 or 5 a.m. and start my day. There's something about that time of day that I adore. It's more peaceful, and greeting the day with some yoga poses is a sacred practice that amplifies my inner joy. Today, I love facilitating the daily 6 a.m. Magical Morning Call with my coaching clients. To be honest, some need to be coaxed, but once they see the tremendous benefits, before long they have transformed a former belief that they're "not a morning person" into a life-changing habit. We are set up for the day, in the right vibration and open to miracles and powerful manifestations.

True happiness comes from within and lasts a lifetime. It is available beneath the camouflage of the outer temporary trappings and indulgences. In my twenties and mid-thirties, I rarely felt happy after a night of partying in some trendy restaurant or club, drinking vintage champagne, dressed in my best outfits. I felt empty and anxious most of the time, although few would ever have known it. Thankfully, I recognized what was missing, a connection with God and my soul. Contrast is a teacher, and this student was ready.

For me, nothing can replace the natural highs I get from having a meaningful conversation that uplifts and supports our evolution or walking in nature—which raises awareness and releases endorphins—or being able to drive myself home whenever I want. I will never miss waiting in the rain for a cab. Best of all is being present with my family.

At home, we began using the happiness principles in our relationships, inviting one another to share three things that went well during the day or telling one another the three things we appreciated about the other, including things we appreciated about ourselves. We labeled our bills and debts "happy bills" and paid them with ease and gratitude. It made dealing with rebuilding our lives so much more enjoyable. We became more conscious of our attitudes and reactions and reminded one another of the benefits of being happy for no reason and every reason.

Consciously practicing happiness habits became a way of doing things, and every area of our lives improved. One of the happiness habits I love is to focus on the good, what's going well in our lives, rather than on what's going wrong. We felt empowered and connected to the flow of positive energy that these valuable life tools brought to our lives.

Spirit is Key

I believe more than before that now is the right time for us to become comfortable saying that we are eternal beings with temporary bodies. There is an accelerated awakening on the planet. You only have to look at the number of books being written on the subject and the teachers worldwide spreading messages of hope and wellness that are satisfying the appetite we have for this wisdom.

Spirit is simply the essence of who we are; it's our nature. The more in tune we become with our unique spiritual essence, the quicker we can tune out the lies we've been told and reveal the truth. You can take control of your life to allow what's longing inside of you to be born. Having a spiritual practice helps us recalibrate and relax back into ourselves with trust and a knowing that we are being guided and never alone.

I've decided to come out of the spiritual closet where I've hidden for too long and share what's been in my heart since early childhood. It has been suggested that spirituality is an instinct of humanity. That means that we have an intrinsic knowing regarding our truth in terms of our essence. We may have forgotten what that is, but the continual events in our lives offer us the opportunity to reawaken to the possibilities that await us when we develop a deliberate relationship with our spirit. Cultivating this relationship has kept me believing in a positive outcome even when my back has been to the wall in a number of challenging situations.

Although I'm grateful for being able to reveal more of myself and my beliefs through teaching yoga and meditation over the years, I've begun to hold a more extensive conversation around spirituality in my workshops, speaking opportunities, and coaching sessions.

Having more awareness of what we are being called to do and be will only lead to more joy and peace for us all. We must find the courage to be our best Self by letting go of our false sense of self and all the old stories that created it. Stand in your power and share what's in your heart without fear of being ridiculed or judged. I've felt trapped and conflicted for much of my life when it came to my work. I often felt that I was only going through the motions. At times, it felt superficial, but I yearned for more depth, meaning, and purpose. I realized I needed to become that person I aspired to be and, as I've said before, trust that many of my tormentors in life have been my mentors.

You hold the key to your freedom, and raising awareness of this fact and how to access that key has become my mission. We must all be on a mission greater than our fears and problems—no more being locked in a mindset of limitation. No more secrets with yourself. It's never too late to start living from your soul. Make the time to tune in, be silent, and listen; let your spirit be free.

Spirituality and Success

I have found that lasting prosperity, abundance, and the most straightforward path to what you may consider inconceivable success in any aspect of life rely almost entirely on the relationship you first nurture with your spiritual essence. Yet, I believe wholeheartedly that many people are missing this key ingredient in their everyday affairs. What good is having a hefty bank balance if you're unhappy, alone, or sick? As I've mentioned in the introduction, I believe we cannot separate spirituality from true success. True success comes when we honor our soul's mission and are of service. What we sow is what we reap. The law of cause and effect works its magic, and we can use this to strive for positive outcomes by our motives and intentions to bask in joy, peace, and abundance.

Looking outside of ourselves for the answers and quick fixes eventually proves ineffective. Spirituality is something that comes from within us, that inner knowing, and no one can give it to us or take it away. Central to success in any area of our lives is ourselves, and we must know who we are and why we are here. We must uncover our skills and be proud of what we are good at without apology or fear of judgment. We must understand that we are here to master life with all of its complexities and know that they are part of the experience. It's time to celebrate who we are.

Of course, you can create some level of success without a connection to your soul, but what I have found is that this level of success may leave you feeling empty. Conversely, you can be spiritually minded without success, and this too can create a void. Most people are raised to believe that wealth or success of any kind and spirituality cannot coexist. But when we are willing to rethink our belief system about these separate concepts and realize that true success comes from within, we feel secure and awake to the infinite possibilities available to us. Our desire to succeed is a primal force inside that wants us to manifest what we desire. True success is in manifesting desires that not only bring us joy and fulfillment but also have a positive impact on others.

Your success will look different from mine and vice versa by virtue of our uniqueness. Knowing the truth of who you are is the greatest success because from this place you can co-create beyond your current circumstances and tap into the invisible power that both resides within and surrounds you simultaneously.

That spirit animating our body is always for continual expression and expansion—it's how we've been wired from the beginning.

Rise Above Religion

Confusing religion with spirituality is causing unnecessary suffering and delays in our evolution. Perhaps, like me, you were taught to fear God or fear breaking the commandments while you witnessed hypocrisy all around you. I felt a snobbery and an arrogance from many of the nuns and priests I met in my youth, and I quickly picked up on that energy. They created separation, a division, and they were unapproachable, which would have been very intimidating to many. My young mind was always curious, and I couldn't understand how God's servants could act with such superiority over others. I'm not saying that all nuns and priests were like that because, thankfully, they weren't.

But here's my point: when you are raised in fear of doing wrong or being wrong and eventually discover that what you've been told is corrupt and distorted by supposed pillars of society, then it gives us a license to run amok and give the proverbial two fingers to church and country.

We have been let down, misguided, and taken advantage of by irresponsible leaders, and before we know it, we're off doing the very thing we were warned against, worshipping the false gods that fall into the categories of excessive pleasures and debauchery in all their interpretations. Understandably, many of us lost faith in our religion and religious leaders long before the many church scandals became public.

Thankfully, there is a movement to reach beyond religion to higher states of consciousness. We are more aware of our essence as spiritual beings and our ability to transcend our darkest moments. Discerning the truth from the lies and rising above religion, dogma, and the inherent divisiveness they try to conceal is a major shift in the direction of a love-centered world. This is a strong statement, but we have to start thinking for ourselves and trusting our innate wisdom to create more and more miracles.

CHAPTER 12

~

HEALING THE WOUND
TO WRITE FROM THE SCAR

*We learn and grow, or we stay stuck and wither
away. But either way, we all arrive at an end.*

I considered authoring this book during those months we
were living in Australia when I was otherwise idle. I made
several attempts, but I never got too far. Then I heard something that changed everything for me. It was a conversation
between Glennon Doyle and Brené Brown where Glennon
said, "Make sure you're sharing from your scars, not your
open wounds."

The truth was that as the weeks turned into months, I felt
more and more wounded. I recognize it was my ego that was
wounded, but I still hurt. Yet, I knew that this was part of my
spiritual growth, all for a higher purpose. It was nearly a curse

to have so much awareness of what was happening yet feel powerless to remedy it.

This is where trust plays a part. As I've already said, the idea to write a book began about twenty-five years ago and was very much influenced by the direction my life had taken romantically. To share our intimate details with the world is a scary thing, and doing it with the intention to serve in some way does not guard against potential criticism or judgment from those who might be offended or see it as an act of vanity. Yet, despite the risk, I trust my decision to fulfill this desire.

Evidence of how truly detached I was from my religious roots was up for scrutiny. Was I brave enough to follow through with my supposed boldness and defy my father and the ideology of the faith in which I'd been raised?

I could have chosen the path of least resistance, avoiding the potential to grow that I so clearly needed, but instead, I chose the path of growth and becoming more. I knew it would not be easy, and I had every reason to let it go, and because I didn't, it has made me stronger, happier, and more creative.

The worst thing we can do is look at our lives with regret and keep wondering what things would have been like if only we'd made a different choice. Once again, we have to trust that the setbacks and disappointments are success turned inside out. Looking for the good and searching for the deeper meaning in the events is the best way to transcend and surrender to the uncertainties.

The irony of uncertainty is that it's certain. It's part of our everyday experience. We don't know what our next thought will be, let alone how much longer we will live in our physical bodies. We cannot predict anything with absolute certainty, but we can set goals with the expectation of achieving them. I believe we can set ourselves up for the best possible outcome by being detached from it. Part of the creative process when it comes to manifesting our goals is in allowing them to come into our experience. There's a caveat we must apply to our goals, and that is to make space for *something even better* to emerge. What a wonderful idea that opens us up to more possibilities and opportunities that we may never have considered.

We learn and grow, or we stay stuck and wither away; but either way, we all arrive at an end. Our choices in life are made consciously and unconsciously, and the results we get are always in line with our levels of awareness. I'm so grateful that I had enough understanding to choose to stay and weather the storms when they came and bask in the sun on those brighter days, of which I have experienced many.

Twenty-five years go by so fast, and the proof of that lapse in time is found in the lines on our faces, and if we're lucky, in the wisdom of our hearts. We need forward momentum all the way, being ready to face the world and deal with our issues and challenges as they arise. When you do the hard things, you elevate your vibration and send a message to the universe that you are a phenomenal being who is not going to let fear slow you or your mission down.

Looking back, I am so glad I followed my heart and chose to show up as a warrior, even when I was outnumbered. Was it worth it? Absolutely! Imagine missing all the many magical moments, the memories shared, and the life we dared. What was such a big deal twenty-five years ago is now just a moment, one that we all could have missed if different decisions had been made. Isn't that amazing to consider?

Personal growth is a choice. Change is guaranteed. Wisdom lies within us all, but that doesn't mean we are wise. I believe our wisdom can only be accessed through deliberate inner work and a burning desire to live a more heart-centered, conscious life. With wisdom comes peace and calmness of mind. As I write, I can reveal that my dear old dad admitted to me less than twelve months ago that he agreed with me that there are many ways to God. I was out walking in the woods at the time when he called me. He was oblivious to the tears that rolled down my cheeks and the swelling of love in my heart as I gazed up at the clear, blue sky in deep acknowledgment of this long-awaited exoneration and acceptance.

CHAPTER 13

REFLECTIONS

Pearls don't lie on the seashore. If you want one, you must dive for it.

—Chinese Proverb

It's All Led to This

Everything I have ever done has led me to this moment, to the work I love, the relationships I cherish, and the appreciation I have for all the lessons. Every day, I aim to be a better person than yesterday and keep starting over just as each moment allows. I choose to always be a learner with a beginner's mindset but with a veteran's wisdom tucked neatly in my pocket for when I might need it.

I no longer see myself as useless. I believe I am good enough and that as a girl from Phibsborough in Dublin with no third-level education but with a passion and desire to serve, I can do God's work any day of the week without question. I am grateful that my dad planted that seed deep within me many decades ago. I know I am God's highest form of creation and an expression of that same God, and I know that everyone on the planet is the same. I no longer feel inferior to anyone and never feel superior.

I accept that not everyone will like me, and I won't like everyone either, but I can love them and keep them at a distance. I am okay with that and feel that not wanting to waste time somewhere I'm not valued comes with age.

Speaking of age, I'm so grateful for the time I've been gifted so far, and while I look forward to enjoying many more trips around the sun, I'm mindful of how sacred every moment is and how important it is to jump on every opportunity to make a difference, to spread love and lift someone higher.

It is true for me that as I have gotten older, I no longer fear death or see it as a grand finale. On the contrary, I see it as a new beginning, albeit in a different dimension. Of course, that doesn't mean that I'd be unfeeling or indifferent when someone I love passes on. I will miss them with all my heart just as I miss those who have already departed. It's helpful for me to believe that we are eternal beings and that we're offered a new way of communicating with our loved ones who have transitioned.

I sometimes reflect on how I'd like to be remembered, not in any conceited or arrogant way but more by way of measuring how much I have lived up to my promise, the one I made before I took on my physical form in this lifetime.

Did I tick all the appropriate boxes, the commitments I promised to keep? Was I a good student and servant? Did I love enough? Did I laugh enough and have fun?

I remember being at a workshop one time, and we were invited to write our eulogies. There was a lot of nervous laughter in the room for a few minutes. Clearly, there were more than me who felt very unprepared for such a task. Nonetheless, the noise subsided, and we got to work with some guidance from our leader. I can't remember exactly what I wrote now, but what I do remember is how it made me feel to do this exercise. It was powerful, and I vowed I would stop making excuses and "messing around" with my life. I reinforce this message frequently to myself, my family, and my clients. It's a great motivator. It boils down to this—you can have your excuses or your dreams, but you can't have both. My husband shared an acronym with me recently: NME, No More Excuses. When you say NME, it sounds like an *enemy*, and that's what an excuse is—an *enemy* of our dreams.

Sixteen Lessons from My Journey

As a learner-leader who is willing to teach and share with others what is possible when you change your perspective on life, I wanted to share some of the most important lessons I've learned on my journey so far:

1. Our soul is intelligent and intuitive. We must learn to trust it when it whispers to us.

Your innate wisdom, which stems from your soul, becomes your ally every day to assist you in solving your problems and guiding you towards the right path. Your heart is home to your soul. You can ask your heart for guidance anytime.

Tune in by getting still. Focus on the energy of your heart and ask a clear question that elicits a yes-no response, then listen. You might hear the answer, or most probably, you may feel the answer in the form of a yum or yuck feeling. You might notice your energy expand as you sense that you've been given a green light to go ahead with your idea, or your energy may contract as you sense that it's not the right time or move. It's a gift to you; be loyal to your soul.

Do you want to continue living stubbornly, defending your point of view, staying stuck and small, or do you want to throw caution to the wind and follow the voice of your soul, trusting that it knows the way?

Our ego is our false self that masquerades as our true Self. It pretends to support and protect us but only keeps us disconnected from the source and our innate wisdom. The ego lives in fear. Knowing this makes it easier to silence the ego. You may have heard the acronym for EGO, Edging God Out. I'd like to offer one for SOUL, as the Source Of Unconditional Love. Let go of your ego and let your soul be your guide.

2. *You are a spiritual being having a human experience.*

You are not your thoughts, you are not your body, and you are not the roles you play. You are so much more than what you see in the mirror. You are the thinker of those thoughts; a spiritual being having a human experience. Amazingly, the invisible, most formidable part of you is untainted by anything you may have experienced that hurt you. That part of you, your soul, remains pure and unblemished. While the soul is untouched by trauma, the connection to the soul can be severed, blocking its light and wisdom and preventing you from seeing your value and worth.

In my work, a considerable part of the healing process begins with reintroducing clients to their higher Self and reminding them that their soul is shatterproof, and therefore, they too are shatterproof. This element in my hypnotherapy sessions has probably had the most significant impact on my clients' return to wholeness.

3. *There is another way to know God.*

As Caroline Myss, who is often described as a modern-day mystic, says, "Religion is the politics of God."

If religion has been a destructive force in your life, *there is another way* to know God.

We were not told that we are the creators of our reality or that we are the most powerful person in our lives. We have been taught to feel separated from one another and God. It often takes a life-changing event or situation to wake us up and search for greater meaning. On this search, we may find another way to know God. There are many names for God. Find your truth and live in alignment with the God of your understanding.

4. *Everything happens for a reason.*

   Everything happens for a reason. As an example from my life, I didn't end up in a convent surrounded by women who dedicated their lives to God in that particular way, even if I only had a brief notion of it. However, I am now surrounded by phenomenal, mission-driven women who are learning to draw from their life experiences and serve humanity in their valued and unique ways.

   As a coach, I am blessed to help these women reach their potential and show the world who they are. I love to help them come out of hiding and show up as their authentic Selves without apology. They learn that having a burning desire is the first step to creating change. They know how to use their imagination and build self-belief. They identify limiting beliefs and change them to get breakthrough results. I have seen them grow in confidence as they acknowledge their gifts and talents and own their place in the world. Many have identified their deeper purpose and changed direction in their careers and businesses while increasing their income tenfold. They learn about the universal laws, set goals, and improve their self-image to make their dreams a reality. Most of all, they learn to trust themselves.

Things work out in the end as long as we do the inner work and recognize the setbacks as signs that something needs to change. When things don't go to our plan, it's because we are not a vibrational match for what we're doing.

5. *You are right where you are supposed to be.*

As a hypnotherapist, I am blessed to liberate individuals from unhelpful mental programming around trauma and abuse and help them to rewire their brains with new beliefs. I like to remind each person I have the privilege to work with that they're doing more than okay and are right where they are supposed to be. Each of us has an amazing capacity for change.

We can only ever start from where we are right now. And right now, you are ripe and ready for change.

It takes a growth mindset and an attitude built for success to help you move through the moment's challenges. Freedom awaits, but not before you are willing to accept where you are and how you got there. Letting go of the past through forgiveness and moving forward is easier with an acceptance of "what is" and a vision of where you're going.

I love these words from Amy Purdy, a three-time Paralympian medalist: "You never know when your detour will lead you to your destiny."

6. *Tap into the Infinite Intelligence to manifest what you want.*

Don't be afraid to want more; your spirit wants to expand and express itself through you. Believe that abundance and happiness are yours to claim without apology and that others do not lose out when you follow your desires. In fact, I believe the opposite is true. Everyone benefits when you follow your desires and claim your right to live your best life.

Ideas come to you because they want to be manifested through you. When we begin to understand how the mind works, we can manifest whatever we want. Your mind is connected to Infinite Intelligence. The mind thinks in pictures. Use your imagination to create a gallery filled with everything you desire and then see and feel it as if you have already received it. Focus on what you want. Believe you deserve it and allow it into your life. We all have our fears, doubts, and feelings of being inadequate. We must retrain ourselves to think differently.

Many people want to see things materialize before they can believe them. As Martin Luther King Jr. said: "Faith is taking the first step even when you don't see the whole staircase." Build your faith muscle through positive, powerful affirmations and gratitude. Affirmations are positive statements. These statements are thoughts. Thoughts are energy and become things. Your thoughts cause you to feel a particular way, and to get what you want, you must feel grateful and happy in the *knowing* phase before you are in the *receiving* stage of manifestation. Trust that what you want is waiting for you and that you have everything within you to achieve it. Get your mind and soul in sync by harnessing your imagination to communicate your motives clearly to the universe and create the space for whatever you want to manifest. Become a manifestation magnet and expect to receive.

I've always had great faith in the invisible realm and an earnest expectation of good things coming into my life. Most people don't trust what they cannot see, and that's the problem. The trick is in flipping this belief around. Trust that what you want but cannot see physically is already here; it's just on a different frequency. You can get on that same frequency when you believe that idea. Don't get caught up in needing to know *how* it's going to unfold; that's where most get stuck and think this manifestation hype is a load of malarkey. It's not. It's a universal law.

7. *Do what you love and ditch the fear.*

Believe you can do whatever your heart desires. Don't be half-hearted; go all in. Understand that fear is an inherent part of the change. Anytime we want to do something we've never done before, fear will raise its head. Fear isn't necessarily a bad thing. It protects us in certain circumstances, such as when we are in danger of an attack or we walk too close to the edge of a cliff. When it comes to pursuing our passions, fear can confuse us and hold us back from making a move that could change our lives. It comes down to our subconscious programming, our belief system. It's the mind's job to protect us and bring us what we want, but if we had a history of failing when it comes to getting what we want, fear will try to block us from further failure, and so we must rise above that way of thinking and not allow that to happen.

Do not wait for the right time to come out of hiding and share your gifts with the world. The right time is always in that moment you realize you want something new. There is never a perfect time. As author Doris Lessing points out: "Whatever you're meant to do, do it now. The conditions are always impossible."

Perfectionism is another word for procrastination, something I'm very familiar with. It's so liberating when you take action in spite of the fear and doubts. Break free from the mental prison held together with old, untrue, outdated, and limiting beliefs that are standing in the way of your greatness. Start before you are ready, and just trust that you'll figure it out.

Luckily, your talents and gifts are not fixed, and there's no expiry date on them either. Remember, your soul has a purpose. It's called dharma. It defines who you are regarding what you do, how you do it, and why. I believe we grow into our dharma throughout our lifetime. When I first began teaching yoga, I knew I was expressing my dharma. I grew so much as a person, mentally, emotionally, physically, and spiritually. I wanted my students to feel the benefits that I was receiving from this ancient practice. What was interesting was how much my dharma evolved because of teaching yoga. It opened my heart and freed my soul, allowing me to express myself further. You know you're living your dharma when what's in your heart is being expressed through your word and deed in service to humanity, without restriction, bringing you and those you serve joy and pleasure.

8. *Invest in yourself.*

I've had many redirections, as I've shared with you throughout this book, but investing in myself with coaches and courses has helped me to develop my confidence and earn a great living consequently. I learned early on that if I wanted something different, I had to do something different and become the person I needed to be in order to attract into my life what I wanted. A lack of financial resources was the usual excuse that I gave myself. Yet, I could always find the money for meaningless socializing, for more clothes than I could wear, and let's not forget the perfume collection. None of which brought me lasting happiness.

Nevertheless, I eventually concluded that I couldn't do it alone. I needed new skills and a new way to look at life. I also had to convince myself that I was worth the investment, and the game changer for me was thinking about where I'd be in a year or more if I didn't invest in myself. Growth doesn't just happen. Seeds of desire need to be planted and nurtured. There needs to be accountability to reach our goals. New habits need to be cultivated so we can stay on track. Being surrounded by like-minded people who are progressive and committed allows for a greater possibility of achieving your dreams.

My first significant investment was in training with Deepak Chopra. Hands down, it is still one of the highlights of my life. The return on my investment has paid multiple dividends, and not all in financial terms. I developed a habit of self-investment, and I know I will continue to do so for the rest of my life as I love learning and growing. It's a hobby and a lifestyle and never bores me.

Most recently, working as a consultant with Bob Proctor and his teachings has taken my business and life to another level. I took a risk when I signed up. It was the single most significant investment in myself I'd ever made, and I didn't have the money lying around. But I learned I didn't need the money until I decided that I wanted to become a consultant. Once I said yes and put my deposit down, the money flowed in as promised. I started this aspect of my business just as the COVID-19 pandemic turned the world upside down. That didn't deter me because I trusted that people wanted to grow just as much as I did, and I was not wrong. As Bob says, you'll never go broke when you invest in yourself. Of course, the investment is more than just money. Investing in yourself involves spending time studying, learning, stretching beyond the norm, and implementing. It includes leaving the herd sometimes and having to set new boundaries to protect your dreams. Decide to go after what you want! The solution to your future lies within you. If you want a pearl, you'd better learn to dive. You will not regret it.

9. *Take responsibility for your attitude and actions.*

A positive attitude is everything. You may have heard that your attitude determines your altitude in life. You have the freedom to choose how you see things. Choice always has two possible outcomes—one that will lead you to joy and the other to more pain and suffering. As a confessed Pollyanna, I tend to look for the silver lining. This allows me to feel inspired and gives me the strength to not give up.

Having a positive attitude helps you to achieve goals and attain success. It increases self-belief and faith in your abilities. It brings more happiness to your life, which ripples outward, enhancing others' lives.

By taking responsibility to upgrade our thinking around our life circumstances, we can create a world with more acceptance, less separation, and more equality and tolerance, leading to an inclusive and diverse society. It begins with you and me. We must be the hero in our own life. We cannot grow unless we study ourselves. We cannot find solutions if we stay focused on problems, and we cannot succeed if we expect to fail. Our attitude is something we can change, and it's comprised of our thoughts, feelings, and actions. The first thing is to think of different thoughts, ones that are aligned with our values and vision. Once we are thinking supportive thoughts, our feelings are positive and aligned. This means we will most likely make great choices that move us to act in a certain way. That certain way is by law, predicting our future. Develop a bulletproof attitude that no other person can destroy.

10. *Lead from integrity, not perfection.*

I am willing to lead from a place of integrity, not perfection. Leading from perfection would be too difficult and misleading and would more than likely prevent me from serving authentically. I've already procrastinated long enough on many of my dreams. Beware, there's a fine line between perfectionism and procrastination. Progress beats perfectionism every time. Just start before you're ready. Commit to serving the world with your brilliance.

Stay true to who you are. Don't allow the opinions of others to dissuade you and show strength in your vulnerability. Many people I've worked with have often remarked on my willingness to be honest and vulnerable about my experiences. The reason I do this is to give people permission to open up, say what is on their minds, and admit their mistakes. Once you share your story, it's as if a huge weight has been lifted, and it's not such a burden. We all prefer to be around people who are honest and genuine. There's enough hypocrisy in the world, and too many get caught up in a culture of comparison. I've learned that when we compare ourselves to others, we are not creating in our own lives. I've also learned, in nearly forty years of working, the importance of meeting people *where they are* by being transparent and nonjudgmental because we all want to be seen and heard. In fact, I heard Oprah say once that the three most important words in the world are not "I love you" but "I hear you." Good leaders listen to hear. We can all listen better.

11. *It's never too late to change.*

Don't tell yourself that you're too old, that you have missed the boat, or that you can't teach an old dog new tricks. I see myself as a late bloomer, if I'm honest. It took me a while to achieve certain things in my life—most notably, becoming a mother at age forty-one and writing this book at age fifty-seven. I was one of the last of my friends to get married too.

It took me decades to grow into the woman I have become, doing what I love from a place of worthiness. At times, I feel that I'm only starting, and that excites me. It gives me energy and inspires me. It makes me feel young.

The present moment is constantly renewing itself, which means you can start afresh at any moment, even if long-term change sometimes requires a long-term commitment. There is no expiry date on your life purpose.

Gandhi told us, "If we could change ourselves, the tendencies in the world would also change. As a man changes his own nature, so does the attitude of the world change towards him."

Simply put, be deliberate in creating change in your life. We must not try to change other people as this is futile. Everyone is responsible for changing their circumstances, and oftentimes, people resist being changed until they are ready.

We each have so much control over our responses to life's circumstances, altering our thinking in the blink of an eye. Accept that change is a constant, even when it's not always welcome or easy to handle. Life offers us the chance to demonstrate resilience, strength, and spontaneity. To quote Richard Bach, "What the caterpillar calls the end of the world, the master calls a butterfly." So much wisdom is found in those words, as I'm sure you will agree. You and I can instigate personal change at the click of our fingers. Draw that proverbial line in the sand and give yourself a fresh start with new rules and the flexibility to change direction as you see fit.

I've said throughout this book that change is inevitable; personal growth is a choice. So, why on earth do we resist change? If that caterpillar resisted change, we'd be deprived of the emergence of the beautiful butterfly. We resist change because of a fear of the unknown, and that applies not only to the negative changes, such as ending a relationship or facing a health scare, but also to the changes we long for, including emigration to Australia, marrying a man who was married before, and so on.

Resistance tries to keep us safe, but it fails. We feel unsafe when we're not growing and feel stuck in settle mode filled with *if onlys* and *what-ifs*. If I had resisted my inner voice's lifelong guidance, I might have fallen out with my father and been a statistical victim of family dysfunction, estranged and bitter. That would have been more painful than biding my time and trusting that the day would come when we would find common ground on our differences. If I had resisted leaving the police force, I might never have seen as much of the world as I have. I may not be as open-minded, having shared wonderful cultural exchanges with friends from all over the world, fulfilling a young girl's dream. If I had resisted changing careers multiple times and overcoming my saboteur, who insisted I had no staying power, I would never be doing the work I love so much. If I had resisted marrying my husband, I might not have had the opportunity of experiencing unconditional love from a genuinely kind and supportive life partner. I may not have learned patience, tolerance, and resilience. I would not have had the pleasure of having two beautiful stepchildren, who have grown into outstanding adults, both of whom I love very much. I would not have been able to witness how love would always find a way to make complicated things easier to conquer. And if I had resisted pursuing my relationship with Declan, I would never have known the joy of being Finn's mother. Resistance lost, and my heart won every time.

Get comfortable being uncomfortable and take those life-changing risks. It's a must if you want something more and something exciting. I know it's scary at times, but so is not ever knowing what life would be like if only you'd faced the fear and taken that next step. You will handle it, trust yourself. A motto to adopt, perhaps: "Say yes to risks and no to regrets."

12. *This too shall pass.*

You may be experiencing something in your life right now where you doubt yourself somehow or have a major struggle. Hit the pause button and step back. Be willing to look through wise eyes. Trust that it will get better. Look for the gift in the challenge. What is it teaching you? Are you paying attention? This too shall pass; it is inevitable. Nothing in this life is permanent, and the only constant in life is change. Nothing good or bad lasts forever. Challenges are as temporary as you allow them to be. Sometimes, we must sit with the discomfort, but know that it will not last forever. The *weight* of your pain will be influenced by how long you *wait* to deal with it. You are stronger than you think, braver than you believe, and more creative than you can imagine. Feed your soul every day and listen closely for its guidance. You can navigate the world more creatively.

13. *Let go of the past.*

One of the most powerful habits to break is thinking that your history defines you. You are not your past or your family's past; you are not your thoughts about the past. You are an elevated being who can think of new thoughts and experience new things. Let any shame end with you; don't carry over your parents' issues. Two of the most powerful words we can use to free ourselves of the past are *let go*. I know it can take courage as you step into unfamiliar territory, but with persistence and dedication to changing your reality, soon your new world will become familiar. It's time to tell a new story and embrace new beginnings. Bow to the past, thank it, and move forward with the determination and passion of a soul released from a mental prison.

14. Make your mess your message.

Everyone has something they wish wasn't there. When television broadcaster Robin Roberts discovered she had cancer, she was reluctant to tell anyone. Her mother advised her to "make your mess your message." She is doing just that, sharing her story of resilience to inspire others going through their own *mess*. We all can turn that something into our greatest gift. In so doing, we are not only liberated from our difficulties, but we hold the key to making the world a better place so that the pain we experience ends with us and may even help others.

When we heal ourselves, we have an opportunity to awaken the light within others. We don't all need to be therapists or healers to do this work. Anyone can do it. Often, a casual conversation with a random stranger can profoundly affect our lives. We each can be that person. Don't make your mess messier by holding on to guilt or shame; use it to make a difference. Be the light.

15. *Forget the problem and find the solution.*

Life is not easy, no matter who you are. You will always face problems. Your ability to cope with such problems makes all the difference. We get hurt, rejected, abused, and ignored. We feel invisible, anxious, and afraid. We tend to become defensive or withdrawn. As long as we remain in these states, we cannot find a solution. Constantly talking about our problems keeps them alive and amplified. Energy flows where our attention goes. This is why so many of us feel trapped and continually focused on what's missing and going wrong.

We must go within to connect with our true Selves, which can be found through meditation, seeking a solution, and the ability to forgive the past. As if by magic, the answers come, and the heart expands. You feel love, compassion, and understanding. You begin to see the innocence in the other. You begin to let go of the problem and understand how you can move forward. Long-awaited ideas emerge from the field of infinite possibilities. Look for loving solutions whenever possible, and if someone rejects your good intentions, send them even more love and light.

Sometimes, we need to put on our big-girl pants and not take things so personally. Everyone is dealing with their own stuff. Apologize when necessary and ask for forgiveness too. Put your hand up, then give yourself a high five for having the courage to end the misery of a hopeless cat-and-mouse game where there are rarely any winners.

16. *Be grateful.*

Saying thank you over and over all day long keeps your vibe high and your heart full. As Meister Eckhart says, "If a man had no more to do with God than to be thankful, that would suffice." I could fill this section with quotes that I love on gratitude, but I'll restrain myself and offer this one from Brother David Steindl-Rast, "It is not happiness that makes us grateful. It's gratefulness that makes us happy."

I've heard that gratitude acts as an antidepressant, producing a feeling of happiness and contentment. When we are grateful, our brain releases dopamine and serotonin, which makes us feel good. If we consciously express gratitude daily, we can strengthen this habit and experience the inherent benefits it evokes.

Gratitude is a practice, and the key to happiness is in our hands. We must learn to be thankful for the gift of being alive and for every moment we get to respond to life's painful experiences and grow. I have a daily gratitude practice that I teach to my clients. It allows us to focus on and expect the good in our lives, and that's usually what we get. Having a grateful heart hooks us up to the universal heart and communicates our appreciation for all we have. Magically, we are gifted more of the same and often something even better.

When we returned from Australia, we had a new appreciation for life and immense gratitude for the opportunity to start over. We were able to count our blessings and feel thankful for all the little things we previously took for granted, such as hanging a picture wherever we chose without the need for a landlord's approval. The more grateful we were, the happier we were, and that picked up speed. We had become human magnets for more good things coming our way. Our businesses began to grow, as did our self-esteem and confidence. In turn, we served with more humility and empathy in all our affairs.

There's nothing quite like having it all one day and gone the next to put what's important in life into perspective. I've experienced it and am so grateful that I did.

Final Words: Don't Die with Regrets

I hope this book will encourage you to follow your heart. I firmly believe that when we follow our heart, we are following God's great plan for us to live an optimal life. None of us knows how much time we have left to play in life. The curtain can come down without warning. It's always better late than never to make a start. I'm sure you don't want to die with regrets either. So, here's what I have to say to that:

Say your "sorry"s and your "I love you"s now. Wear your best dress and underwear to the supermarket. Sing in the shower. Accept sincere compliments with a thank you. Wear your favorite lipstick. Leave everyone you meet feeling better for knowing you. Give the love that you seek. Show your appreciation to those who have helped you. Tip more. Laugh out loud. Lighten up and have fun. Compliment others. Praise yourself. Dance in your kitchen and embarrass your kids. Hug everyone you meet. Listen intently to what people have to say. Sing from the top of your lungs. Apply for that job. Ask for a raise. Be your own cheerleader. See the innocence in others. Start your nonprofit. Open your own business. Run that marathon. Climb that mountain. Move house. Get the dog. Ask that certain someone out on a date. Declare your undying love. Have that child. Marry that person you know is the one. Be seen, be heard, be kind, and leave your mark.

Make space in your life and think, really think, about what you truly want and how you want to live. Remember, it's never too late to change until it is too late. In Bronnie Ware's book, *The Top Five Regrets of the Dying*, she recounts the deepest regrets her patients shared as they approached the end of their lives. The number one regret is, "I wish I'd had the courage to live a life true to myself, not the life others expected of me."

When I read that for the first time, it grabbed me. While I have followed my inner guidance most of the time, I couldn't help but pause to check in on myself and ask whose life I was living. It made me sit up a little straighter. I vowed to recognize how precious time is and how sacred life is.

We are using only a tiny percentage of our potential, and I am driven to expand my own while helping others do the same. As Thomas Edison reminds us, "If we did all the things we are capable of doing, we would literally astound ourselves." We just need the courage to express what's in our hearts and get out of our own way.

I hope you're considering making some significant changes now that you know you have an inner guidance system, a reliable accomplice. No matter what you're going through, there is always another way to handle it. Seek the loving solution. See the innocence in those who are less aware and remain open to miracles.

Above all else, as Dr. Wayne Dyer says, "Don't die with your music still in you."

Success begins and ends with you. If you're looking for that one person who can change your life, look in the mirror.

Define what success means to you. I define success in terms of living in harmony with my core values and my commitment to being of service and how much I'm adhering to that. Many people think that success is all about financial wealth alone. It is not. We all know or know of wealthy people who appear to have it all but who feel lonely and unhappy and therefore would be deemed unsuccessful by many people's standards. I remember having a conversation with a very well-known and wealthy businessman. I was really taken aback at the time when he told me that all he really wanted was to be liked for who he was, not for his fortune.

Don't be led by anyone else's version of success, and don't compare yourself with anyone else either. Comparison is a thief of your creativity and, ultimately, your success. Here's the truth, and I hope it lands on you the way it does on me: you are unique, and you have an infinite supply of your uniqueness. Someone might try to copy you, but they will never sustain it because they don't have access to your personal, infinite, God-given supply of ideas and uniqueness. Every day, attempt to be a better version of yourself than you were yesterday and keep starting over and learning.

Decide where you want to expend your energy. You were born to master your life, capitalize on your strengths, strengthen your weaknesses, and learn from your mistakes. Don't get to your deathbed with regrets. Don't allow the naysayers to bury your dreams with you. Do the thing you fear and trust that the death of fear is guaranteed.

Hell is a place we create from our thinking. We suffer when we believe the lies that we have told ourselves and think we are doomed to endure a life of mediocrity. We berate ourselves and others and continue this endless not-so-amusing merry-go-round expecting things to improve.

Facts don't matter when your dream is big enough. Don't allow the outside circumstances to influence your decisions; follow what your soul wants, and you'll rarely go wrong. Life is precious. Heal the past. Forgive. Pause often. Celebrate your uniqueness and bravely express yourself. Live with intention. Love intensely. As Whitney Houston reminded us, the greatest love of all is inside ourselves. Love yourself unconditionally. Depend on yourself and know that you are designed to create. No more hiding; show up and do you in all your glory. You are enough, you matter, and you're invincible.

I believe when we work on our spiritual Self, it positively impacts our personality, self-image, and attitude towards the world. It sustains us from the inside out and is a permanent anchor holding us in a place of trust to the invisible force that surrounds and flows through us.

Just trust, listen to your heart, the keeper of your soul. It is wise and knows the way.

ACKNOWLEDGEMENTS

I would like to thank my kind and loving husband Declan for his unrelenting support, encouragement and patience in putting up with me for the duration of writing this book and beyond. Thank you to Judy O'Beirn, Marisa Peer, Sarah McLean, Peggy McColl, Susie Moore and Edel Coffey for your encouragement and endorsement of this book; it means the world to me. To the editing team, Judith Scott and Day Bolger for helping me to put the final touches to my story.

To my friend and client Evelyn Mullers, who read my manuscript and offered her expert eye and editing skills (a talent she possesses, unknown to me) and made such a difference to the flow of the sentences. Thank you to Ethna Archer for your feedback on reading the unfinished manuscript, it was very much appreciated.

A special thank you to Sarah McLean for your encouragement and endorsement with this book, it means the world to me.

I would like to thank the great teachers I've trained with and learned from, Deepak Chopra, Tony Robbins, Marisa Peer, Bob Proctor, Lisa Nichols, Elizabeth Peru, Peggy McColl,

Michael Bernard Beckwith and Neale Donald Walsch. Your teachings transformed my life.

Thank you so much to the amazing Marci Shimoff, with whom I trained as a Happiness trainer and who very kindly has written the foreword of this book. I have learned so much from you.

To all the healers, therapists and coaches I've done workshops and had sessions with, thank you. Especially Carolyn Curtis with whom I did my first coaching training. To Izabela Fouere who jolted me into thinking bigger about the possibilities for my life, thank you.

A big thank you to all my clients over the years for your trust in me to be your guide and for allowing me to do the work I love and cherish. You are helping me fulfil my Soul's calling. I trust I have done the same for you.

Thanks always to my wonderful friends near and far who have contributed to my life in so many ways. Your friendship means the world to me.

I would like to thank my wonderful parents, for their love and support throughout my life. I am eternally grateful to my dad for planting the seed that my life had a purpose, it led my search. And mam, you are the glue that holds us all together. I love you both more than words can say.

Thank you to my siblings for the laughs, the tears and solidarity over the years. We are a great team. I love each one of you so much.

My stepchildren who are beautiful, kind and progressive adults now. Johannah and Josh, thank you for being in my life. I love you both so much and am so proud of who you have become. I look forward to many great experiences together.

Finally, my precious son Finn, I love you more than words can say. Thank you for choosing me as your mother and making my dream come true. You have made me the happiest. I am always here for you. Go out into the world and be who you were born to be. Love, believe in yourself, be kind and always do your best. You've got this.

ABOUT THE AUTHOR

Pauline Rohdich is the founder of Phenomenal Results Ltd. and is known as The Mindset Detective. She combines her expertise as a Success Mindset Specialist and her investigative skills, which she honed from her time as a Garda (policewoman). She helps soul-centred women to open their hearts and minds and connect with the wisdom of their life experiences, so they can go from feeling invisible to invincible while living abundantly.

She has appeared on Ireland AM, the Elaine Show, and Today FM. She has been featured in The Daily Mail and Positive Life magazine. Her client list includes the Bank of Ireland, AON Insurance Group, and Salesforce. Pauline has studied with successful icons such as Deepak Chopra, Bob Proctor, Marisa Peer, and Marci Shimoff, to name a few.

All this experience has come together in a way that now serves her clients at the highest level. Pauline believes that getting the life you want doesn't have to be a mystery.

Through a unique combination of services that include spiritual success principles, proven practical strategies, and transformational hypnotherapy, she helps women break free from their limiting beliefs to reach their true potential.

Pauline is an avid reader and learner. She loves yoga, walking in nature, and good food. She lives in Galway, Ireland, with her amazing husband Declan, cherished teen son Finn, and their adorable Golden Doodle, Luna.

To find out more follow the link
to my website below

www.themindsetdetective.com

Printed in Great Britain
by Amazon

84543479R00133